Kat the Dog

Book 1
The Seventh Pup

JO ALLEN

Ky
PUBLISHING

First published in Great Britain in 2024 by Ky Publishing

This is a work of fiction. Names, characters, places, and incidents either are the product of the author's imagination or are used fictitiously. Any resemblance to actual persons, living or dead, events, or places is entirely coincidental.

If you find yourself identifying with one of the villains, Kat suggests you keep it to yourself or your friends might start to look at you differently.

For more information: dogwalla285@gmail.com

Cover and Illustrations by Creative Covers

ISBN 978-1-0686346-0-4 (paperback)

ISBN 978-1-0686346-1-1 (ebook)

www.katthedog.co.uk

In memory of Jim
and our many dogs

Chimera:

An Illusion;
A Fire Breathing Monster

THERE ARE SOME PLACES
ON THIS EARTH
WHERE NOTHING IS QUITE
AS IT SEEMS
WHERE MAGIC HAPPENS

Kymera

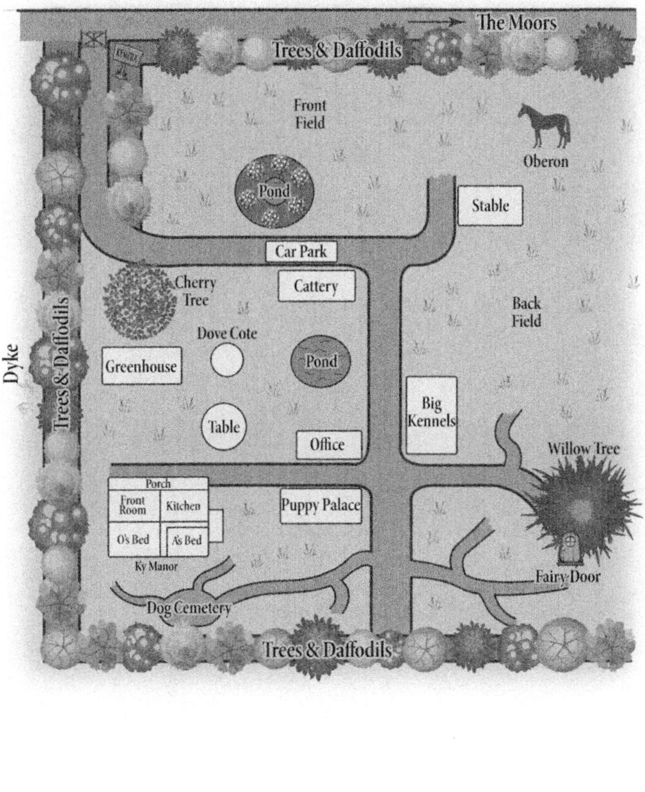

The Moors
Trees & Daffodils
Front Field
Oberon
Pond
Stable
Car Park
Cherry Tree
Cattery
Back Field
Dove Cote
Dyke
Trees & Daffodils
Greenhouse
Pond
Big Kennels
Table
Office
Willow Tree
Porch
Front Room
Kitchen
Puppy Palace
O's Bed
A's Bed
Ky Manor
Fairy Door
Dog Cemetery
Trees & Daffodils

Contents

1. July 7th - Today's the Day 17
2. The Expert Opinion 23
3. Butterflies 29
My Seventh Birthday 34
4. Who the Heck's La Lupina? 38
5. The Seventh Pup 43
6. A Dog to Love 49
My Seventh Birthday 55
7. The Treehouse 58
8. Do As You Would Be Done By, But You'll Never Be Rich 62
9. Duke 69
10. 'Chosen One?' As if 75
11. Feeding the Dogs 81
12. The Paintings 87
13. Back to Me, Me, Me 92
14. Dog Guardian 99
15. Time For a Change? 107
16. The Pup Gets a Nasty Shock 114
17. Who the Heck's Pookah? 119
18. Pandemics and Stuff 127
My Seventh Birthday 131
19. Canine Communication 133
20. Duke's Story 137
21. Night Time Shenanigans 144
22. Miracles Can Happen 150
23. The Past is a Different Universe 155
24. Lupina Tries Out Her Powers 162
25. Any Takers For La Lupina? 168
26. Cousin Felix Comes to Visit 173

27. What's in a Name?	180
My Seventh Birthday	187
28. A Contaminated Dog	189
29. Nick Has Another Shock	196
30. Olivia Goes Hot	202
31. Kat Meets Oberon and a Man Comes to Visit	207
My Seventh Birthday	214
32. Olivia Has a Plan and Archie Gives Her a Present	216
33. Olivia in Love	223
34. A Footling Dandy	228
35. The First Steps	234
36. Kat and Katja Overhear Nick and Felix Talking	240
37. Kat Saves the Day	246
My Thirteenth Birthday	252
38. The Moors	254
39. A Dog Runs Off	261
40. Laurence Brings Some News	267
41. Queenie's Tale	275
42. Archie's Version	283
43. The Dog Inspector	289
44. Positive Thinking and Meeting the Fairies	296
45. A Man with a Briefcase	306
46. Fat Cat Pink Dog	312
47. Archie is Cross and Olivia is Upset	318
48. Queenie is Discombobulated	326
49. Kat Steps Up	331
50. Olivia Has a Plan	338
51. Kat Helps the Plan Along	343
52 A Happy Ending	349
Author Note	353
Acknowledgements	354
Glossary	355

The Seventh Pup

Kat

Hello there, that's me.

My name's Kat and I'm a dog.

Daft, I know, but there you go.

I do speak in rhyme at times, but mainly when I'm chanting spells. Oh, did I forget to say? I'm a magic dog, the seventh daughter of a seventh daughter. My mum, Katja, was a seventh daughter and so am I, which makes me a 'Double Seven'. Double Sevens are very important dogs, according to Queenie, who's my mentor, which is a posh word for somebody who likes to tell you what to do because they know best. She's a Double Seven too and Top Dog at Kymera, where we all live. Double Sevens are rare, but we're not the only two in existence.

Queenie says that I'm the Dog Saviour, or La Lupina, and I've been sent to 'rescue Dogsworld from the tyranny of a growing number of wicked humans', and dogs too, believe it or not. It's because, as well as being a Double Seven, I was born on a special day. I don't understand it all, but I do *feel* quite special, I must admit. Queenie, who's a lot older and wiser than me, is the real boss though. She's my great grandmother and nobody likes to upset her. I know *I* don't.

Queenie

According to Queenie, there's a horrible dog, called Malina, lurking out there somewhere. Queenie's best friend, Duke, says she's out to 'snaffle' me. Queenie's always telling Duke off for saying stuff like that and frightening me. This Malina's not a Double Seven like me and Queenie, or even a Seven, like Mum. She's one of the Sixes. Queenie says Sixes are bad, because they belong to the dark side. And that's *not* good.

Kymera, pronounced *Ky-mere-a*, is our home. There are lots of pretty flowers and trees here, little chickens, ducks and geese, doves, a horse, and some occasionally misbehaving vegetables. It's an enchanting place. And I love it. We all do.

Archie – that's Queenie's human/best friend, who runs Kymera – calls it a Dog Sanctuary, because lots of dogs live here. Apart from our own family, there are dogs who come on holiday and other dogs that Archie's rescued. Most of them are what Queenie calls 'dim dogs', meaning that they can't communicate very well and tend to follow the crowd instead of thinking for themselves. Archie's great though, a 'proper person'. We all love Archie, even though he can be a bit annoying at times. Archie and Queenie are like a real couple. Everywhere he goes, *she* goes. She even follows him to the toilet for heaven's sake.

My human's called Olivia. She's the best. She's Archie's granddaughter and came to live at Kymera after her parents were killed in a car accident on her thirteenth birthday, which is very, very sad. She's coping though, especially now she has me to look after her. She thinks I'm gorgeous and cute, which I get. I know I shouldn't boast, but I *am* kind of sweet. Olivia and I mostly rely on telepathy to communicate, but one day I'm hoping we're going to be able to talk together properly. She has a special relationship with the fairies, who live in the treehouse, high up in the willow tree on the back field. Yes, there are fairies who live on Kymera. In fact there are fairies everywhere, so Queenie says, if only people would open their minds to see them. Olivia is the link between their world and ours, like her mother was before her. Not that she really understands that yet. *I* only know because Queenie told me.

***

Now let me introduce you to the (mainly) Jack Russell gang:

Katja

My mum, Katja, is amazing. She's not a Double Seven, but she is a Seven, meaning that she's 'enlightened' and can talk. That puts her way above the dim dogs. She's Olivia's favourite (or was, before I came along of course). She's Queenie's granddaughter, daughter of Queenie Two, Queenie's daughter. Sound complicated? The trouble is Archie can't always be bothered to think up names for the dogs, so Queenie Two, my gran, got named after her mum. Queenie says, because of that, she's never been 'the full ticket', one of Archie's odd little phrases. I mean all dogs should have their own name, to make them feel special, even if they are one of the dim dogs. Gran's okay though. She just likes food and not much else, apart from a good riot.

Queenie 2

I'm really glad Mum didn't get called Queenie Three or I might have been Queenie Four. In fact, Archie was all for calling me Katja Two, after Mum, but Olivia put her foot down and I got landed with the name Kat instead. I would have preferred Princess, but nobody seemed to think of that. I don't know why. It seems a no-brainer to me. Olivia's always saying that to Archie: 'It's a no-brainer, Granddad.' He just nods and pulls a daft face.

DUKE

Queenie's best mate is Duke. Duke isn't a Jack Russell like us. He's some kind of sheepdog cross. Queenie is sometimes rude to him about it, but Duke gives as good as he gets. He's always winding Queenie up and they have a right good squabble. But that's called 'banter' and is nothing to take offence at. It even indicates that they sort of like each other whilst pretending that they don't. Apparently.

Duke's the designated Dog Guardian. It means he's supposed to look after me and make sure I don't come to any harm, particularly from that Malina one. That's because I'm very important, being La Lupina, the Dog Saviour, in case you've forgotten. Sometimes he doesn't take his responsibilities seriously enough, but he's all right is Duke, even though he does make fun of me a lot. He loves going out with Olivia and Oberon, our resident horse. He and Oberon have an understanding that annoys Queenie. I think she may be a bit jealous. But Oberon has 'hidden depths', according to Duke.

Valentino

Then there's my dad, Valentino, who's only half Jack Russell. He's generally considered a handsome chap, a big hit with the girls with his long, silky coat. Queenie says he has potential. It's a question of unlocking it. Only nobody has found the key yet. Duke isn't convinced that there is a key that will fit. But he may be jealous that Valentino's better looking than him, though he won't admit it.

OLD SOLDIER
(IN HIS PRIME)

Old Soldier, who's a Cavalier King Charles Spaniel, lives in the kitchen, mainly behind the cooker. He used to be a show dog and his show name was King Charles of Kilcragg. He was 'one CC off a champion' (whatever that means) in his day, or so Archie is always boasting to his friends. They look like they don't know what a 'CC' is either and don't like to ask, but Archie says it like it's something very important. They try and look impressed, which isn't easy because Soldier's even older than Archie and looks it. He's actually a hundred and forty, I think. In dog years of course. It's hard to imagine him up on a podium, his brown and white coat shining from all that brushing, eyes glowing with pride as he's presented with the winner's medal. Nowadays he can barely see or hear, his coat's full of knots (Olivia's always cutting them off as she can't get a comb through them), his legs can barely hold him up and he doesn't know what day of the week it is. He doesn't have many teeth, but he still loves a jam butty, preferably strawberry. Archie says Valentino gets his good looks from Soldier, that he must have come to life one day and taken a fancy to Valentino's mum, who has since gone to her forever home. I don't think Archie is entirely sure about that, but I reckon it's true because that would make Soldier my granddad. So it's no wonder I feel like a princess, what with him being a king.

There are my six sisters as well of course, but they don't really count as they won't be staying at Kymera, unlike me. They're only interested in food and playing and are always pushing me out of the way as if I don't matter. They obviously don't realize how important I am. I suspect they all belong in the 'dim' department. They haven't even got names. Olivia says they'll be given names when they go to their forever homes.

POOKAH

And finally, there's horrid Pookah. She's not actually part of our gang. None of us can stand her. She grew up with Nick, Archie's son, and his two sons, Felix and Laurence.

It's hard to think of Nick, Old Nick we call him, as family even though he's Archie's son. Olivia doesn't like him. I'm not sure that Archie is actually that fond of him. I don't suppose you have to like your family though. You're just stuck with them, so Queenie says. I can barely believe Nick is related to Archie, they're so different. Old Nick likes money whereas Archie doesn't care about money at all, which is probably why he never has any. Olivia thinks Nick was horrible with her mum, Jessica, when they were little, and that's the reason Jessica left Kymera and went to live somewhere else. Archie doesn't like to talk about it, so it's all a bit of a mystery.

Olivia really loves her cousins though, Nick's two sons. Felix, the younger one, is jolly and smiley and my mum, Katja, loves him too. Olivia and Felix sometimes argue about who my mum loves the best. Felix knew her first and she's supposed to be his dog. But Felix lives away, studying about food, although he often comes back to visit, to see Archie, Olivia and Mum, and the rest of us of course.

Then there's Laurence. Queenie thinks Laurence is very handsome. And so does Olivia! I've noticed she turns all red when Laurence is around. I think she'd like to marry him really. Only he's her cousin, and Archie seems a bit wary of Laurence. Calls him a 'footling dandy', whatever that is. Archie doesn't half have some funny expressions.

So there's a peek at our little tribe. I hope you'll want to read the first step of our journey. It's called Kat the Dog. And the starring role goes to… you've guessed it. Myself! (But don't tell Queenie. Please.) I wanted to change the title to Princess the Dog, but I got voted down, which seems a touch unfair since I am the main event after all. Still, I'm not one to sulk.

I do hope you enjoy it.

OUR FAMILY TREE

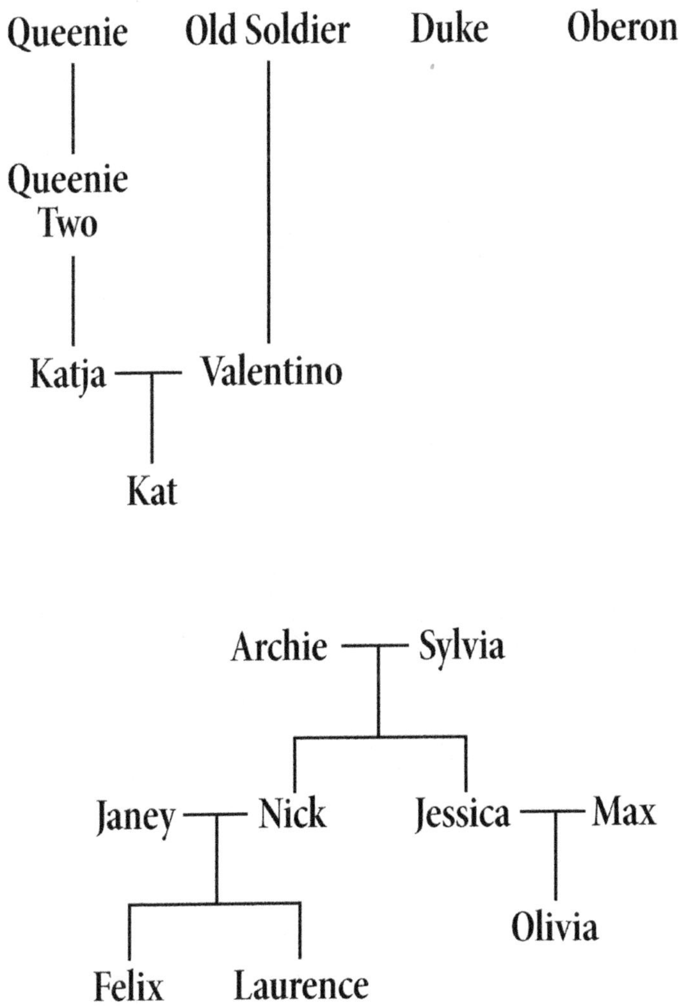

1. July 7th – Today's the Day

Queenie

'What the…?' Queenie, Jack Russell extraordinaire and Top Dog of top dogs, stopped herself saying a rude word, as a tomato flew past her from out of the greenhouse and splattered against the wall of the Manor. As queen, it was her duty to remain dignified, even if the entire crop of tomatoes should suddenly decide to take up flying.

Queenie was in no mood for misbehaving vegetables. That very morning, the mirror in Archie's bedroom had told a wicked lie. Instead of the fine figure of a dog she was used to seeing reflected back at her, she'd been confronted with a positively portly creature, sporting a definite smattering of grey around the muzzle, not to mention several white hairs sprouting from the black patch over its eye. To make matters worse, Queenie was sure she'd overheard the words 'middle-age spread' being bandied about amongst a huddle of dogs as they glanced her way (although they may just have been passing wind). 'It's puppy fat,' she'd bellowed, 'so think on, unless you fancy being turned into a cat.' (Not that such a feat was in her repertoire, but they weren't to know that.)

A garden gnome, sitting with its fishing rod next to the pond, looked up and frowned. 'You can be quiet too,' snapped Queenie. The gnome shrugged and went back to its silent meditation.

She poked her nose around the greenhouse door. The eggs were jiggling about on their tray, the cucumbers were rolling around, bumping into one another, the spring onions were bowing and waving at each other and several tomatoes were bouncing up and down like they were gearing up to take off. It simply wasn't normal behaviour for a bunch of vegetables.

She glanced over to the far side of the garden, where her granddaughter, Katja, was huffing and puffing her way over to the old shed in the corner.

'What are up to, young Katja?' she yelled, as Katja set to digging like a demented ferret.

Fancy! Katja took not a scrap of notice of Queenie and began to dig even more frantically.

Valentino, who had followed Katja over, stood stupidly squinting as earth was flicked into his eyes.

The flowers in the garden opened and closed

their petals, blinking madly at the spectacle of soil flying in all directions, the leaves on the trees launched into a little dance, and another tomato zoomed out past Queenie and landed near the pond. The two bird-brained ducks, Turner and Hooch, who considered the pond their own personal and private domain, tossed their scrawny necks and set off squawking like a couple of hysterical hyenas.

***

Queenie's ears stood on end. Of course! What was wrong with her? Could dog dementia be setting in early? She'd seen the date on Archie's paper that morning. JULY SEVENTH! It just hadn't registered. No wonder Katja was piling on the weight and waddling like a duck. 'Wake up, world,' she barked frantically at the universe and at Archie in particular, who was sitting at the garden table enjoying a jam and cheese sandwich and a cup of tea. 'TODAY'S THE DAY!'

But the universe carried on as if the queen of all canines hadn't said a word.

'Oi, Archie,' she hollered. 'This is Queenie speaking, your lord – or rather lady – and mistress, your wisest of wise companions. Get off your big, fat bottom, you lummox, and do something.'

Archie never even looked up. Though, to be fair, his bottom was neither big nor fat, but actually quite trim, in line with the rest of him.

Queenie might as well have been talking to thin air, to a mirage, to a deaf, balding, daft old coot. But he was *her* daft old coot. And woe betide anybody who forgot it.

'Olivia,' she barked, 'surely *you* can feel it. *You're* a keen Dogwalla. An event of supreme importance is in the offing.'

Olivia, lolling on the grass, buried under a pile of dogs, continued staring at her stupid phone, tutting every so often and frowning. Honestly. Humans!

Even the dogs, Queenie's supposedly loyal subjects, could barely be bothered to lift their lazy heads. Queenie Two, her intellectually-challenged, guzzle-guts daughter, who resembled Queenie both in name and appearance (though, sadly, not in brainpower), blinked a few times and looked around gormlessly in the vain hope that a second breakfast might miraculously materialize.

If an assortment of brain-dead vegetables could get it, why couldn't her nearest and dearest? Had the entire population of Kymera been struck down with stupiditis?

'Wooooh, wooooh,' howled Queenie, as a last resort, at the sun hanging like a fireball in the clear blue sky, before succumbing to a violent coughing fit.

That caught Archie's attention all right. Accustomed to dogs howling at the moon, not the sun, the dopey duffer covered his ears. Then he caught sight of Katja disappearing under the old shed. 'Hmm, that's odd,' he said, standing up and sauntering over there at the speed of an arthritic snail.

Olivia pushed the dogs off, leapt to her feet and dashed after him. She was nearly as tall as Archie now that she was a teenager, slim and slightly gawky, with a wistful face and beautiful sad, green eyes.

Archie stood scratching his head, cap in hand.

'What's up, Granddad?' said Olivia.

'Katja's behaving mighty strangely.' Archie bent down and thrust his hand under the shed before Queenie had time to issue a warning.

Giving a loud yelp, he snatched his hand back out and began rolling around on the grass, flapping it in the air and uttering several words entirely unsuited to delicate canine ears.

'Don't be such a drama queen, Granddad,' said Olivia, laughing.

'Drama king, if you don't mind,' said Archie.

The commotion disturbed the dim dogs dozing in the garden, who leapt to their feet, yapping idiotically, and raced over to see what was happening. Nitwits, with barely a brain cell between them, they piled on top of Archie, and started licking his face and hands. He could probably have *done* with a wash, but this was neither the time nor the place.

'Pack it in, you lot,' yelled Queenie as Archie staggered to his feet, muttering and cussing.

The dogs jumped up and down, barking their silly heads off.

Katja remained stubbornly under the shed.

And that was the start of the day that Dog History was made.

2. The Expert Opinion

KATJA

'That dog really likes the sound of its own voice. Yap, yap, yap,' said Archie to Olivia as they both stood staring at the old shed. 'Sometimes I feel like throwing a bucket of water over her.'

'Poor Queenie. She was only trying to get your attention, Granddad, that's all.'

'Hmm. I take exception to my baggin time being interrupted by that blarting duffer.'

Olivia did a quick eye roll. *Blarting duffer*? *Baggin time*? Sometimes it was like Granddad was speaking a foreign language. Still, they couldn't stand there all day *like cheese at fourpence*, another of Granddad's little sayings that made no sense. 'I can manage, Granddad,' she said. 'You go inside and give that hand a wash. It doesn't look like she's broken the skin though.'

'Well, it still hurts, Olivia,' he said, pulling his dumb glum face. 'You think she'll come out from under the office for you and not for me, do you?'

'Yes, I do. Go on, off you go, Granddad,'

said Olivia, making shooing movements at him as she bent down to stare into the murky depths beneath the shed. 'Come on, Katja. You come out for Olivia, darling,' she wheedled.

'You don't think that stupid voice is going to do the trick, do you?' said Archie, stomping off to the kitchen, chuntering about know-it-all little girls.

Olivia shook her head. 'Yes, actually.' Little girl indeed. She was thirteen years old, a teenager. And she probably knew as much about dogs as *he* did, possibly more.

***

She sat down on the grass beside the 'office', Granddad's name for the ramshackle building in the corner of the garden that everybody else called 'the old shed'. Stuffed with yellowing papers curled up at the edges, it housed a cluster of spindly and not-so-spindly spiders rather than a pile of well-ordered documents and a neat row of pens. She only ever ventured in on a strictly *need to enter* basis.

'Come along out, Katja. There's a good girl. You know you want to. There's no point hiding under there, now is there?'

Slowly slowly, Katja inched her way out, fat

tummy dragging on the ground, and crawled towards Olivia, whimpering slightly.

'What is it, Katja?' said Olivia, smoothing her hands over the two, oddly misshapen, black patches either side of Katja's soft white coat. 'Oh, I see. I was thinking maybe you'd started to take after your mum, scoffing everything in sight. But you're going to be a mum yourself, aren't you? How utterly wonderful. Silly Granddad. He should have realized.'

Katja nodded her pretty head and gazed meaningfully at Olivia with her warm brown eyes.

'We understand each other, don't we, you and I?' Olivia ran her finger down the brown stripe on Katja's nose, which spread out over both eyes, giving her a startled expression. 'Come on, let's go and tell Granddad the good news.' She scrambled to her feet and smoothed down her best 'I Love Dogs' T-shirt. 'There we go, darling,' she said, scooping Katja up in her arms and marching towards the kitchen.

***

As they came through the door, Archie's mouth dropped open.

'It's just Katja, Granddad, not ET. No need

for that daft look.'

'My, what a little pudding,' he exclaimed. 'When did *you* turn into such a fatty, young lady?'

'Been breeding dogs a long time, have you, Granddad? A hundred years or so, is it?'

'A hundred and five, if you don't mind. Just approaching my prime.'

Archie stretched out his arms and took hold of Katja, who whined and grunted as she was poked and prodded, tipped this way and that, turned upside down and back to front.

'Well I never, young lady,' said Granddad finally, after putting on his specs and having a long hard peer at her belly, 'you've turned into quite a barrage balloon on the quiet, haven't you?'

Katja gave a few short, sharp barks as she tried to struggle free.

Archie put her down on the floor, where she gave herself a good shake and glared balefully at him, sighing and grunting like a grumpy little pig.

'And that's your expert opinion, is it then, Granddad?' said Olivia. 'Honestly, you only have to look at her. You must have had an inkling, surely. I mean, I can tell and I'm only thirteen.'

'Aye, thirteen going on thirty.'

He pointed at Katja, who was rolling on her back as if trying to draw attention to her condition. 'Look at that. No shame. Only three years old and already getting herself into bother. What's the world coming to?'

'That *is* twenty-one in dog years.'

'That's no excuse. Standards are slipping. Wouldn't have happened when *I* was a boy. So, who's the daddy?'

They both turned to look at Valentino, who was fast asleep, feet twitching, lying on his back on a raggedy old chair, a likely feasting ground for moths. He opened one eye and swished his fluffy tail back and forth. His long silky, brown and white coat, so different from the short, smooth coats of the other Jack Russells, made him a big hit with the girls. And he knew it.

'He looks very pleased with himself,' said Olivia.

'Hmm. Doesn't he just?' said Archie.

Valentino blinked underneath the locks of hair semi-obscuring his eyes like a horse's forelock, upped the tail-swishing and curled the corners of his mouth.

'He looks very smug.'

'Dogs can't look smug...' said Archie '...unless they happen to be called Valentino perhaps.

'Anyway, these pups are coming at just the right time.'

Olivia looked at him quizzically.

'Money's just a bit tight, that's all, love. Nothing for you to worry your pretty head about.'

3. Butterflies

'Right! Puppy Palace,' said Archie. 'Let's get this show on the road.'

Puppy Palace? Ha! Peeling paintwork, rusty bars and dirty windows were all that was left of the once Royal Residence, built by Archie for the mothers-to-be and their pups. Age and life had taken their toll on Queenie's old pal, who now struggled to keep abreast of even the day-to-day tasks.

Archie had always liked fresh air, more than was good for any living creature, striding around Kymera, beating his chest and taking in great lungfuls of the stuff. Even in the depths of winter, he'd leave his bedroom window wide open at night, much to Queenie's annoyance. She'd often creep under the covers to keep warm and lie next to Archie, who could snore his way through a nuclear attack, no trouble, window open or shut. Poor Queenie was the one who had to keep her ears open for any nocturnal squabbling coming from the Puppy Palace, fortunately within barking distance of the Manor.

Nowadays more of a shelter for down-and-outs, the Puppy Palace was hardly the ideal place for a VID (Very Important Dog) to be making its entrance into the world.

But then a stable's no palace either. And look how that worked out.

***

Rushing around Archie's bedroom, Olivia gathered up a pile of old jumpers used for the dogs' beds, although she was always catching Granddad wearing one or other of them himself. *Honestly, those jumpers are supposed to be for the dogs, not you, Granddad.*

She felt giddy with excitement at the thought of all the little puppies about to be born. Thrusting the jumpers at Granddad, she practically shoved him out the kitchen door and pushed past him, Katja in her arms.

Despite there not being a single cloud in sight, thunder rolled overhead as they walked in single file down the path towards the Puppy Palace. The rumble was soon replaced by an explosion of sound that filled every corner of Kymera, as if all the birds in the world had decided to sing at the same time, in glorious harmony. Olivia gazed heavenwards and was dazzled by the image of the sun rotating faster and faster in the clear blue sky. It was as if God himself, in need of some amusement, had set it spinning with the flick of a finger, like a record on a giant turntable. The enormous rotating yellow globe seemed to be focusing its rays directly down on to the Puppy Palace, which looked almost like a real palace, bathed in a light of pure gold, with turrets shimmering in the deceptive glow of the sun's radiance. A flurry of brightly-coloured tiny entities darted around the entrance as Queenie and Valentino stood stationed at either side, like guards awaiting the arrival of a royal personage.

Olivia came to an abrupt halt and stared at the little creatures, memories of her seventh birthday and her first ever visit to Kymera flooding her mind. She ducked automatically as a flying tomato narrowly missed her head. 'Hey, did you see that, Granddad?'

Another tomato came whizzing towards them and it was Archie's turn to duck, only not quite in time. 'Oi!' he yelled, looking around, red juice trickling down his cheek. 'What the heck are you doing, whoever you are?'

Katja began to struggle in Olivia's arms. 'Katja's getting restless, Granddad. Come on, I think the pups are on their way.'

'Right, let's get her settled. I'll deal with the invisible tomato-thrower later. Just let me get my hands on them.'

Olivia carried Katja into the Puppy Palace, laid her gently on the straw-filled bed in the corner of one of the kennels and carefully covered her over with the pullovers.

'I think we'll just leave her to it,' said Archie. 'She'll know what to do.'

'Can't we watch, Granddad? I've never actually seen puppies being born before.'

'Best not. It might put her off. We'll check on her in a bit. I don't know about you, but I could murder a cuppa.'

***

'The Puppy Palace looked different, didn't it?' said Olivia to Archie, who had a faraway look in his eyes as they sat round the kitchen table drinking tea.

'Different? How d'you mean? Or are you talking about the butterflies?'

'Hmm.'

'The butterflies come out when there's new life on its way. That's always been the way at Kymera.'

'Butterflies…?'

'That's right, butterflies.' Archie nodded vigorously.

'Butterflies. OK. If you say so, Granddad. But what about the flying tomatoes?'

'Flying tomatoes…? It'll just be kids messing about. You know what they're like. I don't know, the youth of today.'

'Well, where are they then?'

'They've obviously done a runner. Don't want to be caught.'

'Hmm,' said Olivia, looking pensive.

7 Years Earlier
My Seventh Birthday

My seventh birthday started out just like my thirteenth, with the promise of a surprise.

The difference was that you and Dad were both still alive at the end of the day.

***

'Happy Birthday, dear Olivia,' you sang as you burst into my room with Dad that morning. 'Hurry up. It's time.'

'Time for what, Mum?' I was still half asleep. Time to get up? Time for breakfast? Time to open my presents? What?

'Time for you to meet Granddad Archie, silly,' you said, clapping your hands. 'Seventh birthdays are special. We're going to Kymera.'

'Really?' Now I was wide awake. I leapt out of bed and ran over to hug you and we danced around the room, whilst Dad looked on, smiling. Remember, Mum? You'd told me so much about Granddad and his dogs. And now I was finally going to meet them all.

The car journey seemed to take forever. I tried desperately to keep awake, but my eyes simply wouldn't stay open. I kept drifting in and out of a world of talking dogs, winged horses, fluttery, fairy-like figures and Granddad Archie saying, There's no such thing as magic, Olivia. Horses can't fly. Dogs can't talk. Fairies are only butterflies in disguise. It's all in your imagination.

I was vaguely aware of you and Dad chatting in the front. Are you ready for this, Jess? I heard Dad say to you. Archie will be so pleased to see you. I can't wait, Max, you replied. I've really missed him. And he so needs to meet Olivia. After all, what happened wasn't his fault. I should have come back sooner.

You never did tell me what kept you away from Kymera for so long, Mum.

And now you never will…

***

'We're here, Olivia, we've arrived,' you said eventually. 'Wakey wakey.'

My eyes sprung open and I jerked my head up in time to glimpse a decrepit old sign propped up against a five-bar gate, a line of barely legible purple letters spelling out 'KYMERA'.

As the car bounced its way slowly down the driveway, I held on to the front seats, straining to see out of the windows. Rows of bright yellow daffodils leaned in on either side, greeting us with nods and smiles, bowing and waving like we were long-lost friends. I waved excitedly back at them. 'Look at all the lovely flowers, Mum,' I said. 'They seem really pleased to see us.'

'They always are,' you said, turning to Dad and smiling.

Tall trees stood like guards, towering over the daffs, camouflaging the ditch on the right and the big field on the left.

'Nowhere in the world smells as good as Kymera,' you murmured, breathing in the delicious fragrance of wildflowers that wafted through the car's open windows.

'Are we coming home?' I said without thinking, and you turned to look at me. 'That's right, Olivia,' you said. 'We're coming home. Clever girl.'

They're all still there, you know, Mum – the daffodils that seem to flower all year round, the trees, the dogs, the doves, the ducks. Everything you loved. Granddad...me...

And the driveway's still full of potholes.

***

Finally, the car bumped to a halt at the end of the drive and the busybody geese came bustling out of the circle of trees, hissing loudly like they always do, necks outstretched, hoping for the chance to give someone a good peck. Not me, I thought, as I slipped out of the car and raced off, my little legs propelling me like a bullet from a gun. 'Where are you, Granddad? We're here,' I cried, as I shot off towards the Manor, past the Cattery on one side and the Big Kennels on the other. Following my instincts.

'Wait for us, Olivia,' you shouted.

No fear. I'd waited long enough for this moment. I was seven years old and on the verge of entering a whole new, magical world, where nothing could ever go wrong. But then I was only a child and life seemed perfect.

Now, of course, I know better. I know that things can go very wrong indeed.

4. Who the Heck's La Lupina?

Katja looked guiltily at Queenie as she lay on her side puffing heavily. Truth be told, Queenie was feeling mad and still a little stupid, more annoyed with herself than Katja for not having noticed her condition earlier. Normally Katja, not one for secrets, would tell Queenie everything, being unable to talk to her mum, Queenie Two, who struggled to grasp anything that didn't directly relate to food.

'Well?' said Queenie sternly.

'Sorry, Gran. At first, I thought I was just putting on a bit of weight and I didn't want to draw attention to it. I do like to keep a trim figure, like you.' Katja blinked her pretty eyes artlessly as she snuggled down amongst the old jumpers.

'Hmm,' said Queenie, somewhat mollified. 'I suppose Valentino's a handsome lad, with those big brown eyes of his and that long silky coat. Between you and him, and with my genes in the mix, you're bound to produce some real good-looking pups.

'Anyway, anything happening down below?'

'Only a rumble or two, Gran. I think it might

just be wind.'

Queenie put on her extremely serious face. This was extremely serious stuff. 'I don't know if you're aware, but *you*, young Katja, *you* are about to give birth to the most important arrival in Dogsworld since…well, my own, as it happens.'

'Really? Am I, Gran? Am I, really?' Katja's eyes grew wide with astonishment.

'Trust me, Katja. You will become a legend in Doglore. A huge honour has been bestowed upon you,' said Queenie grandly. 'You have been chosen to be the mother of La Lupina.'

'La Lupina?' repeated Katja, looking perplexed. 'Who the heck's La Lupina?'

'Really, Katja, your education is sadly lacking. La Lupina is the Dog Messiah of course, destined to save both humans and dogs, well mainly humans, from making an even bigger mess of the world than they've managed so far. Long overdue in my opinion.' Queenie nodded wisely.

'What's wrong with the world, Gran? I like the world. And I love Kymera, especially now Olivia lives here. Life's good. Isn't it, Gran?' Katja shifted about in her bed, trying to find a comfortable spot.

'We can't just think of ourselves, Katja. There is a world beyond Kymera, you know. There are some wicked people out there.'

'Well, Archie's not wicked. And Olivia's not wicked.'

Queenie didn't like being put on the spot. She thought for a moment. 'What about Old Nick? He's not a very nice man.'

'No, I don't like *him*. But is he wicked, Gran? After all, he's Archie's son. How could Archie's son be actually wicked? I mean, Archie's so…'

'Yes, that's enough, Katja,' snapped Queenie. 'The point is La Lupina is on her way.'

'And I'm going to be this Lupina's mother? Are you sure? I don't *feel* that special.' Katja gave a big sigh as she heaved herself to her feet and had a waddle round her kennel before flopping back down again.

'You're my granddaughter, Katja,' said Queenie. 'Of course you're that special. Now, will you be all right? I'm parched, so I'm just off to see if there's any tea left in the kitchen. We'll talk later. Would you like me to send Valentino over while I'm gone? For moral support?'

'NO. Absolutely not. I can't stand the way he looks at me, like a lovesick parrot. I don't want him pacing up and down, getting on my nerves,' said Katja with a shudder.

'What about Queenie Two then?'

'Oh no. Keep Mum away. She might decide to snack on the puppies if she gets peckish. You know what she's like.'

'Good point,' agreed Queenie.

'I'll be fine on my own. Really, Gran.'

'All right, if you're sure. I'll be back soon. You do what comes naturally. It's a doddle once you get started. I've done it lots of times.'

'Thanks, Gran. I'm getting a bit of pain now. Feels like I want to poo,' said Katja, licking her belly.

Queenie nodded knowingly. 'Oh, that's normal. It'll be over before you know it. Just you remember, Katja, you've one very special guest in there.'

***

Queenie ambled over to the kitchen, all sorts of stuff running through her mind. If La Lupina was about to make her entrance into the world, then La Malina would surely not be far behind. According to Doglore, the two of them came as a pair, Good versus Evil. Perhaps she was already here? Queenie needed to have a word with Duke, her best mate. He was well up on Doglore even though he often pretended otherwise. Bob, Archie's best mate, after Queenie of course, was due a visit and he always brought Duke with him. She'd summon him. That's what she'd do.

'I call upon the powers that be,

To beckon Duke to come to me,' she intoned in a low growl as she pushed open the kitchen door with her nose.

'And make it snappy,' she added.

5. The Seventh Pup

'What are you grumbling at, Queenie? Want a cuppa tea or something?' said Archie.

'Course I do,' barked Queenie. 'Do you really need to ask?'

'I think that means she does. What d'you reckon, Olivia?'

'Queenie always wants a cup of tea, Granddad. Do you really need to ask?'

'Sometimes I think that girl understands me better than the old codger,' said Queenie to nobody in particular.

Archie bent down to pick up her bowl, filled it half way with tea out of the pot and put it down in front of her. 'There you go, old girl.'

'"Old" …? Speak for yourself,' muttered Queenie. 'And I'd have preferred a fresh brew and a full bowl.' Still, tea was tea, and she began lapping eagerly.

'Still grumbling? What's up? Are you after a top-up?' said Archie, holding his jam butty in one hand as he leaned down and poured what remained in the pot into Queenie's bowl. 'Spoilt rotten, you are.'

Queenie was relishing her second cuppa,

making it last in case Archie forgot to make a fresh brew, when a little red face materialized at the kitchen window as another suicidal tomato launched itself at the Manor. Splat, splat, splat. The kitchen window was starting to resemble the scene of a grisly murder as a battalion of flying red missiles joined the fray.

'What? Are they back again?' said Archie to Olivia. 'Oi, I'll be having you, whoever you are,' he yelled, standing up and walking over to the window, his face nearly as red as one of said tomatoes. 'Clear off. They'd best not be my *prize* tomatoes you're throwing around willy nilly.'

'Come on, Archie,' barked Queenie, abandoning her tea and making a dash for the Puppy Palace.

Archie looked at Olivia, dropped his jam butty and, tomatoes forgotten, scurried after Queenie, Olivia right on his tail.

***

Thunder banged and crashed in the cloudless sky, as the three of them arrived to find Katja stretched out on the straw, panting with exhaustion, surrounded by little bodies. The jumpers were scattered about the kennel, looking like they were resting after a fight.

'Well I never,' said Archie, gasping for breath. 'You *have* been busy, Katja. That's quite a collection.'

Katja gave a few feeble wags of her tail as she sighed loudly, her eyes fluttering shut.

Olivia opened the kennel door and stroked her head. 'Poor baby, you must be tired. Who's a clever girl, then? One, two, three, four, five, six,' she counted. 'Wow. Good for you, Katja. No wonder you want to sleep.'

'I think that must be the lot now,' said Archie.

***

Kat

Wrong! What about the most important pup of all? Yes, me! I'm not one for complaining, but it's been a rough old ride so far. Grim, and getting steadily grimmer. And now it looks like I'm being abandoned before I've even begun.

The day began with me feeling all cosy and comfy inside my mum's tum, dozing away, enjoying the peace and quiet, disturbed only by the occasional jiggling about and mutterings from afar.

Then the trouble starts.

Out of nowhere, there's suddenly a lot of action going on. I feel myself being shoved and jostled, little legs jabbing me willy-nilly in the eye and sharp claws being thrust up my nose as I'm propelled to the back of a rather long queue. The cheek of it!

'Hey. It's dark in here. Let me out. I'm suffocating. Stop shoving, you lot,' I yell.

But nobody's listening. Nobody cares.

Suddenly everything goes quiet. There's no more shoving, or little legs poking into my tummy and into my face. I try slowly inching forward in the murky darkness but I'm not getting very far. Hours and hours seem to pass. My poor head's beginning to swim and I've no strength left to fight against the others and push them out of the way. That's when I realize that there *are* no others in front of me. I'm on my own in the dark and I don't like it one bit. I feel overcome by tiredness as I lie there, weak and helpless. Then I hear voices, which seem to come from a very long way away.

'Please don't leave me in here on my own. It's very dark. And I'm very tired,' I say weakly, hoping that somebody will hear me.

And somebody does. The alarm is sounded

by a lot of barking and commotion, followed by nasty poking fingers, which arouse me out of the stupor into which I've slowly been sinking. Suddenly – whoosh – I'm propelled at high speed and land - plop - out into the world.

Oh, look, it's so small. It *is* still alive, isn't it? I hear someone shriek. It looks like a dead mouse.

To be honest, I'm not over-thrilled by that remark.

And, as if that isn't enough to finish me off, I'm then subjected to a most humiliating experience before I've even had chance to take my first breath.

I can dimly hear squeals and barks and then rough hands begin rubbing me up and down.

Don't hurt it, Granddad, I hear.

Belt up, the lot of you, says a gruff voice. Not you, love. I mean the dogs. I know what I'm doing.

It seems nobody's listening as the hysterical racket carries on and on. As does the extremely unpleasant rub, rub, rub. No fun at all, let me tell you.

Stop it, Granddad.

Bark, bark, bark, bark.

Save the pup, Granddad. Please don't let it die.

Bark, bark.

All this noise is hurting my poor ears. I just want it all to stop so that I can sleep. No chance of that as the nasty rubbing gets more violent. It's a wonder I'm not rubbed clean away. To top off this nightmare, I then feel hot, smelly breath being blown into my nose. And not just once. Over and over. Eventually I give a cough and the rubbing and blowing finally stops.

Bliss.

And… it's a girl, says the gruff voice. Pup number seven's a girl. It's the runt. It'll do well if it lives, this one.

Weak and feeble as I am, I don't take too kindly to this remark. It doesn't sound like much of a compliment, and I decide then and there that I'll show them and live, even if it kills me.

Here you are, love. Give the little blighter a bit of TLC.

I'm suddenly nestling in a pair of soft, velvety hands.

It's the best feeling.

Like I'm where I belong.

6. A Dog to Love

'What's that noise, Granddad?'

A loud booming and crackling filled the skies. 'What the…?' said Archie, stepping out of the Puppy Palace to see what was happening.

Olivia followed him out and they stood and gazed in awe and wonder at the kaleidoscope of vivid colours streaking across the bright blue horizon. Reds, greens, oranges, purples, blues and yellows, every hue imaginable, flashed and sparkled, sizzled and popped, lighting up the sky in a dazzling array of luminosity.

'Oh wow. That's amazing,' said Olivia. 'Are they shooting stars, Granddad?'

'You can't get shooting stars in the day. Somebody must have let off some fireworks, that's all.'

As Olivia felt the steady breathing of the warm little body in her hands, she knew that Granddad was wrong. 'Welcome to the world, gorgeous,' she said. 'You're obviously a very special little girl.'

***

Olivia was filled with a mixture of joy and sadness as an image of Mum and Dad filled her mind.

She pictured the three of them sitting round the table at home, Mum talking to her about getting a puppy one day soon, maybe off one of Granddad's dogs, possibly Katja. They'd chatted about the kind of puppy she might like. As she gazed down at the tiny creature she was cradling, her heart gave a lurch. It was exactly the kind of puppy she would have chosen. Mum and Dad would have loved her too. She could actually feel their approval.

Even before the accident, Olivia had felt lonely. Other girls at school called her 'strange', or a 'weirdo' when they were being particularly cruel. She lived her in own imaginary world, full of talking dogs and flying horses, unicorns and fairies. She wasn't into clothes and make-up like the other girls and she wasn't interested in their talk of boys and who was going out with whom. There was only one boy that she'd ever felt attracted to and that was her cousin Laurence, Uncle Nick's son. Even as a little girl. Her heart did strange things when he was around. Nobody else ever came close.

She did have one friend she'd known for as long as she could remember. Ariel used to call Olivia's mum Auntie Jess and her dad Uncle Max. But even *she* rarely got in touch these days. She was supposed to be coming up to stay, but she hadn't even answered Olivia's last two WhatsApp messages. Olivia had tried to ring her, but Ariel hadn't answered.

She gave a big sigh.

'Penny for them, love.'

Olivia glanced up at Granddad.

'Penny for your thoughts.'

'Oh, I was just thinking about the dogs, and this pup, and about Mum and Dad.'

'Oh, aye? Don't you be getting all maudlin on me. This is a good day.'

'No, it's just that before, well, you know, the accident…'

'We don't want to be thinking about that now, do we?'

'No, what I mean, Granddad, is that we talked about me getting a pup of my own. And I was just thinking about the dogs here.'

'Well, there are certainly plenty of dogs here to keep you busy.'

'I mean a special dog, Granddad, one that's really mine, like Queenie's yours. She follows you everywhere. It's like you can read each other's thoughts.'

Granddad smiled and looked down at Queenie, who was gazing up at him. 'Yes, she's a grand little dog, our Queenie, one of the best. But you've got Katja.'

'I know, and I really love Katja. She helped me such a lot when I first came to live here. She used to sit under the old willow with me, you know, when I didn't feel like talking or eating. It was Mum's special spot you said. Remember?'

'Course I remember, love. How could I forget? I carved that little door for her at the bottom of the tree, when she was about seven. Her 'fairy door' she used to call it. *And* I built that treehouse for her. Anyway,' Granddad cleared his throat and fiddled with his cap, 'it's time I got cracking again. Those kennels won't clean themselves. Best put that little pup back in with Katja. It looks like it's going to need feeding up to me.'

Olivia stood outside the Puppy Palace cuddling the pup a while longer, thinking about how much she yearned for a special friend.

The trouble with Katja was that she really belonged to Cousin Felix, Uncle Nick's other son, and he could come back from catering college any time and take her away to live with him. And then Olivia really would be devastated.

Then there was Valentino of course. He was sweet and wagged his tail a lot. He often lay next to her on the bed. He did his best, bless, but he didn't understand her the way Katja did.

Even Queenie Two, the canine dustbin as Granddad called her, sometimes came to sit and stare up at her, but mainly when she was hoping for a titbit. Although she had once brought a biscuit and laid it at Olivia's feet, which was a huge honour.

And Old Soldier, of course. Olivia could remember Mum talking about Soldier, who was only a pup when she was a girl. A handsome King Charles spaniel in his time, his once silky coat was now all matted and knotty and, no matter how much Olivia combed him (she was the only one who did), those knots would not budge. He spent most of the day at the back of the cooker keeping warm and popping his head out now and then to see if there was a jam butty (preferably strawberry) going spare. Granddad joked that Soldier was *just approaching his prime,* like him, even though he was practically an antique. Soldier, that is, not Granddad. He said Valentino got his silky coat from Soldier, that he must have come to life one day and made a play for Val's mother, who'd since been adopted by a nice family. But then Granddad had a habit of making stuff up. *Never let the truth get in the way of a good tale* was another one of his sayings. Old Soldier occasionally ambled over to Olivia and slobbered over her hand, which was well-meant, if not exactly pleasant.

***

What Olivia really longed for was a dog that was hers alone to love, one that she could take everywhere with her, who'd sleep next to her at night, like Queenie did with Granddad. It might help fill the hole gouged into her heart when Mum and Dad left her. How could an empty space hurt so much? Sometimes she felt like stuffing the void full of old T-shirts or cut-up rags, but there weren't enough cut-up rags in the world to fill it. She always went to sleep hugging a pillow, but it only dulled the ache slightly. And a pillow wasn't a real live thing. She felt a tear trickle down her cheek.

If she asked very nicely, maybe, just maybe…

My Seventh Birthday

I turned the corner and a fairy-tale castle seemed to spring out of the ground, its silvery towers reaching high into the clouds. Granddad stood framed in the entrance, enveloped in a misty glow, wisps of grey hair poking out from the sides of his cap, looking exactly like his photo on the sideboard at home.

I always loved that photo, Mum, where Granddad has his arm around you and you're gazing up at him. You were probably only about seven when it was taken, the same age as I was then. How long ago it all seems.

I ran up the steps and leapt into Granddad's arms, feeling his whiskery face wet on my cheek as he murmured into my hair, 'Olivia, my little Olivia. Happy seventh birthday.'

'Oh, thank you, Granddad,' I said. 'I've been dying to meet you.'

'Me too,' he said, clearing his throat. 'I think we're going to be great friends, you and I.'

'That's daft,' I said. 'You're my granddad. We can't be friends.'

'Oh, I think you'll find we can, Olivia. You'll see.'

He was right. I mean, what did I know?

As he put me down and went to hug you, I

realized that there wasn't a castle there at all. Just a ramshackle old building with cracked windows and a door hanging off its hinges…

***

A cute little brown and white dog seemed to appear from nowhere, sitting at Granddad's feet. 'Say hello to Olivia, Queenie,' he said. Queenie lifted one paw and held it out, cocking her head to one side. So sweet, with that black patch over her left eye, giving her a funny lopsided appearance.

Whilst you grown-ups all chatted away, Queenie jerked her head at me and set off down the path past the Big Kennels to the back field. I followed, struggling to keep the little stumpy tail in sight as Queenie's pace quickened.

'Wait, Queenie,' I shouted as I stumbled and fell on to my knees. Ow, ow. I did my best not to cry even though it really really hurt, Mum. But Queenie was straight there, licking my scraped knee with her smooth, soft tongue. The sharp sting of pain stopped instantly and the graze began to fade until it disappeared altogether. You always said that dogs have a healing tongue, Mum. And you were right. It felt just like magic.

I never did tell you all that happened that day. I wasn't sure you'd believe me. And you were always telling me to be careful, so I thought you might be cross that I'd done something so dangerous. It became my little secret. I can tell you it now.

Queenie led me to the massive tree looming dark and forbidding in the far corner of the back field. She looked at me and then looked up. That's when I spotted it, nestling high in the branches. I was sure it was your treehouse, the one you always talked about. So up I climbed, clinging fiercely to each branch, until I arrived in front of a little door, a bright purple dragon carved in the centre of it. Sitting astride a branch, I gave the door a push with my free hand, but it refused to budge, so I tried knocking instead. The door swung open, releasing a host of tiny creatures, spreading and fluttering their delicate, brightly-coloured wings. Faster and faster, they swirled around my head, making me so dizzy that I lost my grip on the branch. I felt myself slipping and cried out to you in fear. Mum, Mum. Help! Please. I don't want to die. My dress billowing round me, I shut my eyes tight and waited to hit the ground. Instead, I felt myself floating on a cushion of air, little voices chanting in my ears, Olivia, Olivia, we've been waiting for you. Happy Birthday, Olivia. You're safe with us.

When I finally dared open my eyes, I was sitting with my back against the tree, Queenie at my side snoring softly.

7. The Treehouse

Would the treehouse still be there? She ought to go and take a look, satisfy her curiosity. Finding herself at the foot of the old willow tree, Olivia gazed up into its branches. They looked like they reached almost to the sky. There didn't seem to be any footholds to start her off. She'd probably need a ladder. She didn't remember having this problem when she was seven. Maybe she was braver then.

It was a warm sunny day and she was wearing too many clothes - jeans, T-shirt, baggy jumper. She was beginning to sweat, or glow, Mum would have said. 'Horses sweat, gentlemen perspire, ladies glow, darling'. Olivia smiled at the memory. She struggled out of the jumper, pulling it over her head and throwing it on the ground at the foot of the tree. She ran her hand through her shoulder-length hair to smooth out any knots and gave it a shake. That felt better.

Granddad kept a lot of stuff in the stable next to Oberon's, along with all his tack and bales of straw and hay. There may be a ladder in there, but it was doubtful. She glanced over to see Oberon grazing nearby. 'Oberon,' she shouted. 'Come here, Oberon.'

Oberon lifted his head, shook his mane, whinnied, and galloped over to her.

Olivia pressed her face into his glossy, black coat as she patted and stroked him. 'Do you think you can help me, Oberon?' she whispered in his ear. 'I want to climb this tree and I can't reach.'

Oberon nodded and folded his front legs underneath him so that he was kneeling on the ground. Olivia climbed on to his back, balancing gingerly as he slowly stood up. She felt like a circus performer, only she wasn't sure that she'd last upright for very long if he decided to take off. She grasped one of the branches and pulled herself on to it.

'Cheers, Oberon,' she said, and Oberon whinnied before putting his head down and going back to eating grass.

As Olivia made her way up the tree, branch by branch, she pondered on Oberon doing her bidding like that. Thinking back, she realized that he always seemed to understand what she was saying to him. The two of them had the best time racing over the Moors, often accompanied by Duke, when he was visiting Kymera with Bob, Granddad's best mate. As Granddad often reminded her, she'd never had a riding lesson in her life. It just seemed the most natural thing in the world. She managed to leave her heartache behind when she and Oberon were flying along at a fast gallop, the wind in her hair, through green fields and down winding tracks, stretching for miles. It was like they were one entity. Sometimes she imagined a horn sprouted from Oberon's forehead as he took off into the air, propelled by a pair of wings that had mysteriously grown, the fields below becoming smaller and further away until they disappeared completely. That couldn't really happen though. Because horses didn't grow horns. And they certainly couldn't fly. She never mentioned the flying part to Granddad in case he thought she was 'a sandwich short of a picnic', another of his quaint little sayings.

If only she could understand what the animals were saying though, like they seemed to understand *her*. That would be really ace.

She reached the top of the tree and there was the treehouse, looking smaller and shabbier than she remembered. But, then again, it *was* nearly seven years ago. She could barely make out the purple dragon now. It was all sad and faded looking. She pushed on the door, but it was if somebody had glued it shut, using the strongest glue possible. Then she tried knocking, like she had when she was seven.

Nothing. She waited. She shut her eyes and

willed it to open. She counted to three and peeped through one eye. Nothing. Whatever had happened when she was seven years old, there was no sign of life now. Maybe she *had* imagined the little creatures that saved her life and carried her down to earth. After all, magic was for children and she was thirteen now, practically a grown-up.

No, magic didn't really exist. It was time to put these childish thoughts behind her.

With a sigh, she climbed down the tree, careful not to fall this time. Oberon looked up at her as she reached the bottom branch. Olivia slithered with a bump astride his back and, her hair streaming behind her, held on to his mane as he set off at a gallop across the field.

8. Do As You Would Be Done By, But You'll Never Be Rich

Olivia hadn't had the best night's sleep, dreaming about the little pup, who was struggling to feed off Katja as her greedy sisters pushed her aside. They were only a couple of days old, but she was so much smaller than the others. Olivia woke to find herself drenched in sweat and rolled out of bed. She glanced at her phone. It was nine o'clock already. Granddad would be coming in soon for his baggin. He'd be expecting a cup of tea and a jam butty.

As she staggered into the kitchen in her nightie, he came through the door.

'What? Still not dressed? What time d'you call this to be getting up?'

'Sorry, I didn't sleep very well,' muttered Olivia.

'The animals still need looking after whether *you've* slept well or not.' Archie marched over and put the kettle on himself and then sat down at the kitchen table and picked up his paper.

Oh dear, it didn't sound like Granddad was in the best of moods. Olivia put some loose tea in the pot. Granddad didn't approve of teabags - *Modern rubbish, you can't beat a proper cup of tea, made with proper tea leaves.*

'Strawberry jam and cheese, Granddad?'

'Aye, that'll do nicely,' Archie replied, putting on his specs.

Olivia took the bread out of the bread bin and spread the butter thickly the way Granddad liked it, although he was really supposed to be watching his cholesterol levels. He liked the jam on first and then the cheese sliced on top.

Soldier emerged from behind the cooker. He always seemed to know when there was a strawberry jam sandwich in the offing.

'There you are, Granddad.' Olivia handed him a plate with the sandwich cut nicely in two.

Archie picked up one piece, tore it in half and put it in his mouth, handing the other half to Soldier, who chomped on it gratefully with his gums.

Olivia filled the teapot with hot water from the kettle and put on the old-fashioned cosy knitted by Granddad's mother and placed it on the table next to him. She took a deep breath. 'Will you be selling *all* the pups, Granddad?'

Hardly daring to breathe, she turned back to the sink and tried to look as if she was concentrating on washing up some mugs.

Archie paused before answering. 'We're struggling, Olivia. These pups will bring in some much-needed cash. We can't survive on fresh air. And your Uncle Nick will be wanting his cut.'

'But he never *does* anything, Granddad. *You* do all the work.'

Archie came over to the sink and picked up a couple of mugs Olivia had put on the draining board and shook the drops off, before setting them down on the table and pouring some milk into each of them. He put one spoon of sugar into Olivia's cup. He'd recently cut out sugar altogether himself. It hadn't been easy, as everybody on Kymera could testify to.

'That's the way I like it. That way I know everything's been done properly. Besides Felix comes down to help when he can.'

'Yes, and you slip him some money.'

Archie opened his mouth to say something.

'Don't deny it, Granddad. I've seen you do it. I really like Felix, but Uncle Nick should be paying him, not you. It's not fair.'

'Life isn't fair, Olivia. You, of all people, should know that. Never mind about other folk and what's fair and what's not fair. You think for yourself and do as you would be done by.' Archie poured some tea into the cups from the pot. 'Come on now, drink up.'

Olivia sat down at the table and raised the cup to her lips. '"Do as I would be done by?" she said. 'What does *that* mean?'

Archie looked down at his feet, where Queenie was pawing at his legs. 'Oh, sorry, Queenie. I forgot about you,' he said, pouring half the tea from his cup into her bowl and topping it up with cold water. 'It means, Olivia, Do unto others as you would have them do unto you. In other words, be a proper person. "Archie, my boy," my dear old mum used to say, "you do as you would be done by and you'll not go far wrong." A wise woman, my mother. I think it comes from *Alice in Wonderland*.'

'I don't think so, Granddad. Not the one I've read anyway. And has it worked out, this DoAsYouWouldBeDoneBy thing?' Olivia pulled a sceptical face as she took a sip of her tea.

'Listen, Olivia. I may not live in a posh house with a *Rolls* parked in the drive, but I can sleep at night, knowing I don't owe anybody anything and haven't done anybody a bad turn. You can't say better than that.'

'A "*Rolls*"? Don't you mean a *Porsche*? Or a *Jag*? Anyway, I thought the electricity company was after you for unpaid bills?' Olivia raised her eyebrows.

'Pfft, that's nothing. They're always after

somebody, that lot. No, you do the best you can every day of your life and you'll be rich in things other than money.' Archie opened his arms, gesturing around him.

'But…?'

'It's the simple things that matter in life, Olivia – the sun shining on the pond, the dogs frolicking in the fields, *you* riding over the Moors on Oberon…'

'You're always calling Oberon "that stupid nag". And you're always shouting at the dogs to "BEHAVE". You…'

'Yes,' interrupted Archie. 'It's the simple things in life.' Leaping to his feet and cavorting round the kitchen, tea slopping over the sides of his cup, he burst into song. 'Will you, won't you, will you, won't you, will you join the dance? Will you, won't you, will you, won't you, won't you join the dance?'

'You're silly, Granddad,' Olivia said, laughing, as he put down his cup, grabbed hold of her hands and dragged her round the kitchen with him, her nightie swirling like a ball gown.

'Will you, won't you, will you, won't you, will you join the dance?' they both sang, although only one of them was actually in tune. Olivia thought it best not to mention Granddad's frequent claims to having been the star choirboy in his youth.

The dogs hanging around the kitchen decided they didn't want to be left out either, except it was more jumping about and barking than singing and dancing. Queenie and Valentino, who were somewhat more advanced than the rest, got up on their hind legs, making a lovely couple as they joined paws and danced in time to the music.

'Anyway,' said Archie, sitting down and catching his breath, leaving Olivia to dance on her own with the dogs, 'that's enough of all this frivolity. Some of us have got work to do. You go and get dressed and get yourself out on the daft old nag, whilst I clean out the kennels. You can come and feed the boarders with me later if you like.'

'Really, Granddad? Are you not joking? Can I come and help? Really?' Ever since she was a little girl, Olivia had wanted to help Granddad in the Big Kennels, but he'd always refused. I'm off to feed the dogs, he'd say. Can I come too? she would plead. Please, Granddad. Not this time, he always replied. One of them might turn on you. We don't want to be taking any chances.

'Aye. Now get yourself dressed before I change my mind.'

9. Duke

Duke

'Archie, Archie,' shouted a voice from the garden.

What now? Olivia could have done without any interruptions. This was her first serious attempt at cooking. She couldn't stomach lamb chops and salad. Again! Granddad loved them, that and roast chicken. A pizza with a vegetable topping would make a good, healthy option. She'd rolled out the pizza base, which wasn't looking completely round, but never mind, and lined up a few stray veg that had been lurking at the bottom of the fridge. She was planning on them sitting down to eat it once she'd helped Granddad feed the boarders later.

The kitchen door burst open and Bob came stumbling in, a black and white sheepdog in his arms.

'What's happened, Bob? Is Duke hurt?'

'Where's Archie, Olivia? He's got to help our Duke. I think he's been shot. It's his leg. He crawled in the house this morning and collapsed.

He's alive, but he's spark out.'

'Put him on there, Bob' said Olivia, sweeping the pizza base and uninspiring vegetable offerings on to the floor.

Queenie Two pounced, unable to believe her luck.

'Granddad, Granddad, come quick,' shouted Olivia as she dashed over to the Big Kennels, where she knew he'd be busy cleaning out the runs.

'What's up?' he said, peering out through the bars of one of the kennels.

'Duke's been shot. Come on, Granddad. He needs your help.'

***

Archie examined Duke's leg, feeling up and down like a vet would do. The leg was sticky with blood and, when he pressed one particular spot, Duke yelped and opened his eyes for a moment.

He put his ear to Duke's chest and frowned.

'Get the whisky bottle, Olivia,' he said, 'and the sharp knife out of the drawer. Come on now, quickly. This dog's lost a lot of blood. Pass me the scissors too. And put the kettle on. No, you do that, Bob. We need boiling water.'

'Whisky?' stammered Olivia.

'Yes, whisky,' he snapped.

All right, all right. Manners don't cost anything. Granddad ought to practise what he preached.

'Come on, Olivia, this is an emergency. Fetch me those scissors.'

Olivia grabbed the whisky bottle out of the cupboard and fumbled in the drawer until she finally located the scissors right at the back.

Bob poured some water into the kettle and put it on the hob.

Archie snatched the scissors off Olivia and began cutting hair away from Duke's leg.

'Right, whisky,' he roared, holding out his hand, like a surgeon performing a real operation. Bob handed him the open whisky bottle and Archie poured some over Duke's leg. 'Disinfectant,' he said.

Duke flinched slightly but didn't even open his eyes.

Then Archie forced open the corner of Duke's mouth, poured in a good dollop and rubbed Duke's throat till he swallowed. 'Anaesthetic,' he said.

Finally, he took a slug himself and put the bottle down on the side. 'Courage,' he said, quickly washing his hands under the kitchen tap and shaking the drops off. 'Right, get the sharp knife, Olivia, and you pour some boiling water on it, Bob. We don't want the dog getting an infection. Come round here and hold his head, Olivia. This is going to hurt.'

Olivia held on tight to poor Duke's head, wincing as Archie yelled, 'Knife,' grabbed the steaming implement off Bob and began to cut a hole in his leg.

'Granddad!' she yelled.

Duke merely opened his eyes and closed them again.

'Got it,' said Archie eventually, grasping what turned out to be a bullet between his bloody thumb and forefinger and holding it up triumphantly. 'Now we want a bandage and some cotton wool out of the bathroom cupboard. We need to stop this bleeding.'

'Thanks, Archie, you're a life-saver,' babbled Bob. 'I just didn't know what to do, who to turn to. You know how fond I am of him, Archie. He's such a faithful lad is our Duke, but I just can't take him out like I used to. He deserves better. I've neglected him. I've not even brought him down to play with your Queenie for weeks. And they're such good mates. Thanks, Archie. You're a true pal.'

'Stop your yattering and fetch me that bandage,' said Archie.

Duke was still unconscious but breathing more deeply as Archie carried him over to the Puppy Palace, his leg bandaged up, and laid him down in the kennel adjoining Katja's. He patted him roughly on his head and Olivia gave him a hug and covered him over with one or two jumpers that were lying around.

'Have you reported it to the police yet, Bob?'

'No, but I will do. Not that they'll do owt.' He leaned in towards Archie. 'I wonder, were they after our Duke or were they after robbing me?'

'What would they want with Duke? He's a nice old lad, but he wouldn't fetch much. Mind you, I can't see you being a prime target either. Have you actually got owt worth pinching?'

'A darn sight more than *you* have,' said Bob.

'Is that so?' said Archie, giving him a shove. 'Well, maybe you're right. What I've got, nobody can pinch. The precious things in life. Isn't that right, Olivia?'

'If you say so, Granddad. Although it might be nice to have a smart telly, instead of that old…'

'Fiddlesticks. You need to be out in the fresh air, not…'

'That's a grand set of pups you've got there, Archie,' interrupted Bob, peering into the next kennel. 'You should make a bob or two with them.' Katja gave a warning growl as Bob opened the door to get a better look. 'Hey, what's up with you, Katja? I thought we were friends.'

'They're only three days old, Bob. Katja's protective, that's all. It's only me and Olivia she'll allow near at the moment. Anyway, I can't stand around chit-chatting all day. It's time to get those boarders fed. Are you coming, Olivia, or what?'

'Are you letting Olivia help you feed the dogs, Archie?' said Bob, taking off his cap and running his hand through his thinning hair. 'Never known him let anybody do that before, Olivia. You're highly honoured.' Bob pushed his bottom lip forward and gave her the thumbs up.

'It's time,' said Archie, nodding slowly. 'Right, old boy, you rest now.' Archie patted Duke and ushered Olivia and Bob out, shutting the kennel door behind them. 'We'll come and have a look at you later, Duke. Though why you've ended up here, I don't know, I'm sure. Unless…'

10. 'Chosen One?' As if...

Queenie was worried. She and Duke had been friends for as long as she could remember. He could be annoying at times, but he was one of the few she could have a proper conversation with.

'What have you been up to, Duke…?' she said, pushing open the door of his kennel with her nose, '…getting yourself shot like that? Again!'

Duke's eyes flickered open. 'My leg hurts, Queen.'

'Leave it to me,' said Queenie, as she began to chew at his bandage to loosen it. 'Good job my Archie's never done a course in first aid, otherwise he might have learned how to tie a proper knot. There we go...' She pulled off the bandage with her teeth and proceeded to lick Duke's wound until gradually the jagged edges knitted together and you could barely see where the bullet, or Archie's knife, had been.

'That feels grand, Queen,' said Duke. 'You're not as daft as they say.'

'As who says? Who says I'm daft? I'll turn them into little mice and put them in with the dopey cats. That'll teach them.' Queenie stopped her licking and glared at Duke.

'I'm only messing, Queen. Anyway, I didn't know your magic powers stretched that far. Thought they'd gone rusty, with you not having had occasion to use them recently.'

'Well, I summoned *you*. And here you are.' Queenie preened and drew her shoulders back.

'Oh, cheers. Did you arrange for me to be shot as well?'

'Course not. That must have been the work of La Malina.'

'La Malina…? What are you on about? I bet you just recited your little spell and forgot to say please.'

'Ah,' said Queenie.

'You did, didn't you?' Duke shook his head. 'You know very well that nothing irritates the powers that be more than not being asked nicely.'

'Never mind all that. And actually, it's been so long since there's been any magic round here, I'm prepared to admit that you turning up here may possibly, only possibly, be a coincidence.'

Queenie put her head first on one side and then the other, a sure sign she was on the verge of engaging in a spot of serious thinking.

'Except…' she said at the moment Duke's eyelids had begun to droop. 'D'you know what, Duke? It was when Olivia first came here, when she was seven, that I felt things were starting to happen again. And then nothing. Now she's back. And…'

Duke yawned loudly, and rudely in Queenie's opinion. 'I need to sleep. I'm poorly. Remember?'

'You can sleep any time. This is important.'

But Duke shut his eyes and promptly started snoring.

Queenie tutted, a hundred and one thoughts going round in her head. Maybe the summoning spell had worked after all. Maybe her powers were waking up. Duke turning up like that could well be the hand of Fate.

'Dog Guardian? Why me? La Lupina. Dogsworld…'

Queenie put her ear close to Duke's mouth to hear what he was mumbling in his sleep in between the snores. 'La Malina…' Mutter, mutter. '… Old Queenie.'

'Old Queenie?' she repeated, in horror. 'Who are you calling "Old Queenie?"'

'Well, you ain't no spring chicken, Queen,' said Duke, opening one eye and shutting it again.

'You're supposed to be tired. Get back to sleep before I chew your other leg off,' said Queenie crossly.

'Come on, Queen. Don't be like that. Give a

lad a break.'

'Do you think you've been sent, Duke?'

'Sent where, Queen?'

'Here, you nincompoop. Here. To protect La Lupina. You were muttering her name before, talking about being the Dog Guardian. And you mentioned La Malina.'

'Well I'm delirious, aren't I? Under the influence. Never tried whisky before and I don't care if I never touch another drop. I know nothing about this Lupina one. Or La stupid Malina. I mean I've heard of them, obviously. What self-respecting dog hasn't? But everyone knows it's just a made-up story.'

Queenie inclined her head towards the kennel next door. 'La Lupina's in there right now, Duke. She's actually here at Kymera. The chosen one.'

'Get away,' said Duke. '"Chosen one", my arse.'

'Er… bottom, I think you mean to say, Duke.'

'OK. "Chosen one", my bottom,' said Duke. 'If La Lupina's in the next kennel to me, I'll eat my tail.' He looked round and immediately tucked said tail safely between his legs.

'Listen, Duke. Seven pups were born in there. Seven. You got that? Born on the seventh of July. The seventh day of the seventh month, Duke. And then there's the year. 2023. Add those numbers up and what do you get? Seven again, the sacred number, the number of perfection.'

'Coincidence, Queen. Coincidence.'

'And is it coincidence that the seventh pup just happens to be the seventh daughter of a seventh daughter? Queenie Two had seven pups, all bitches. Katja was the seventh. And all Katja's are bitches. Not a lad amongst them. It's written in the stars, Duke. That last pup is "the one" - the seventh daughter of a seventh daughter, born on the seventh day of the seventh month of year seven. I bet even that Jesus bloke couldn't top that. No disrespect.'

Duke looked decidedly unimpressed. 'It sounds like a load of old cods to me.'

'Cods? I assume you mean codswallop. No way.'

'Cods, codswallop, poppycock, call it what you like. Listen, Queen, I don't want to be rude, but you're delusional. Just because you can perform the odd trick, it don't mean one of your offspring's offspring's offspring is some sort of Dog Saviour. And I ain't no Dog Guardian.'

Queenie's sense of relief that Duke had survived the shooting was fading rapidly. 'We are the elite, you and I, Duke, and it's up to us to keep La Lupina out of the clutches of La Malina.'

Duke began turning round and round, making himself more comfortable amongst the old jumpers. 'Not listening, Queen.'

'Duke!' said Queenie sharply. 'As leader of the pack, I'm appointing you second-in-command, official Dog Guardian.'

'No need, Queen. Especially when there's nowt to guard.' Duke yawned.

'Stop yawning, you dunderhead,' yelled Queenie, her coat practically bristling with pent-up frustration. 'We can hardly leave it to the likes of Valentino, or Queenie Two, now, can we? Valentino possibly has potential, but he's not there yet. As for Queenie Two…I know she's my beloved daughter, but…'

'…she's one of the "dim dogs", if not the dimmest dim dog, probably on the planet,' said Duke.

'There's no call for that kind of talk, Duke. There's nothing wrong with the dim dogs. I know they're not great thinkers and tend to follow the pack, but they're quite a nice bunch on the whole, especially my Queenie Two. She may not be as bright as some, but there isn't a malicious bone in her body.'

'And, I repeat, I'm no Dog Guardian. Now let me sleep.' Duke sighed deeply.

'Ignoramus, you'll see,' murmured Queenie, turning her back on him in a huff.

11. Feeding the Dogs

It was five in the afternoon and Olivia and Archie were in the dog kitchen, a small corner of the Puppy Palace with a sink and a cold-water tap, where Archie washed up all the dog bowls every day. Olivia was wearing her very oldest clothes, some tatty jeans and one of Granddad's rescue jumpers. 'I finally get to help you feed the dogs. It feels like a rite of passage, this, Grandad. It's exciting.'

'"Rite of passage", is it? Get *you*,' Archie laughed as, using a long stick, he began stirring a mixture of cheap cuts of meat and tripe in the old boiler in the corner. The concoction had been simmering away all day on low. He picked up what looked like a large washing-up bowl and began to scoop dollops of it out and pour it into a trough that was sitting on an old trolley, grimy with dirt, its wheels all rusted and creaky. When it was nearly full, he picked up a pair of ancient shears lying close by and began chopping up the meat and tripe.

'It's a bit pongy, isn't it, Granddad?' said Olivia, holding her nose. 'It smells even worse than usual. It's not gone off, has it? It's not going to poison the dogs, is it?'

'It's only the tripe. There's been more tripe than meat lately. You'll soon get to love the smell.' Archie breathed in deeply and out again, making a *haaah* noise. 'The dogs can't get enough of it.'

'I don't think so, Granddad. It smells rank.' Olivia wrinkled up her nose.

Ignoring her, Archie opened the fridge standing next to the boiler and took out a big heap of raw bones. 'Seeing as it's a special occasion, our dogs can have a treat today. They love a raw bone.'

'Isn't that dangerous? I read it could pierce their intestines.' Olivia liked to think she was well up on all things dog-related.

'Poppycock,' said Archie. 'That's only if they're cooked, which makes them brittle. They thrive on raw bones *and* raw meat in fact. I daren't give any to the boarders though. The last thing we need is a bunch of squabbling dogs.'

Archie scooped out a bucketful of flake maize he normally fed to the chickens from a big, oak barrel in the opposite corner of the Puppy Palace and mixed it in with the meat and tripe.

'Should they be having that, Granddad? It's chicken feed, isn't it?'

'You've a lot to learn, young lady. This is all good nutritious food. They love it.'

Lastly, he placed several piles of misshapen,

metal bowls on the trolley, along with a large pewter container filled with water from the sink. 'Right,' he said, 'we're ready for off. Here, put these gloves on. You'll be needing them if you're going to be handling the bones.'

Reluctantly, Olivia pulled on the gloves, which looked like they'd been savaged by a pack of wild dogs at some point in their existence. Archie pulled the trolley to the Puppy Palace entrance and stopped. Taking a couple of the bowls, he dug them in the food mixture, bringing them out nearly full. 'Give one of these to Katja and one to Duke. And check their water bowls while you're there. And I dare say they wouldn't say no to a bone apiece too.'

Duke and Katja seemed delighted with their dinners as Olivia put the bowls down and gave them both a pat. They snatched the bones out of her hand, Duke burying his under a pile of jumpers and Katja hiding hers in the corner behind the dog bed. Olivia spotted the little pup lying apart from the others and gave it a quick stroke before picking it up and placing it back with its sisters.

'Come on, love,' said Granddad. 'The dogs will be wanting their teas.'

As they arrived in front of the Big Kennels, home

to the boarders and the lost dogs that had been dumped at Kymera, it struck Olivia how hard Granddad had to work each day of his life. Like everywhere else on Kymera, the Kennels were sorely in need of a complete refurb. Cracked windows, broken wire mesh hanging loose and peeling paint made everywhere look shabby. Poor Granddad simply didn't have the time to think about such things, never mind do anything about the state of the place.

It was the first time that Olivia had been properly inside the Big Kennels. She'd been in the entrance before, but never allowed any further. Granddad was very strict about that. As he pulled the trolley into the corridor, there was an outbreak of strident barking from dogs on either side, sometimes two, or even three, per kennel. Granddad stopped outside each one and made up as many food bowls as were needed, opened each door and handed them out. Then he topped up the dogs' water from the container.

'Can *I* feed some of them, Granddad?'

'Aye, all right.' He handed her two full bowls and pulled the trolley forward so that she could open the kennel door and put them on the floor. The dogs ignored her as they dived straight in. Then she did the same on the other side.

'I'll do these next few,' said Granddad.

'Why?'

'They're vicious. We don't want you getting bitten.'

The dogs were jumping up at the bars and barking ferociously as Granddad tipped the food on the floor for them and then poured water into their bowls through the bars.

'I'm not scared, Granddad. What kind of dogs *are* they?'

'Staffies mainly, probably ex-fighting dogs. They've been abandoned. It's not much of a life for them here, but I imagine it's better than what they had before.'

'Let me go in with them. They're probably frightened.'

Archie hesitated, but then handed her a bowl of food, stopping in front of a kennel with a lone dog, a large brindle Bullmastiff that stood staring at the two of them.

'He's called Cliff. Don't look him in the eyes, Olivia, and don't touch him. Just go in and put the bowl on the floor,' said Archie. Olivia opened the door and stepped inside. The dog walked round her in a circle, its hackles raised, faintly growling. It was nearly as tall as she was. Archie stood watching the pair of them. Olivia felt the briefest frisson of fear, but then she bent down and placed the bowl on the floor. 'There you are,

Cliff. Enjoy your tea.'

Cliff sniffed at her and then turned away and began devouring his food.

Olivia gave a sigh of relief as she came out and bolted the door.

The rest of the dog feeding was completed without incident. Olivia felt elated at the end, like she'd passed some kind of test.

The last dogs to be fed were Queenie and the rest of the house dogs, but Archie always saved the best cuts for them and of course Old Soldier always got the tenderest pieces of meat on account of him only having his gums to chew on.

12. The Paintings

'I'll tell you something now, Olivia,' said Granddad, when they were back in the kitchen having a cup of tea. 'That Cliff has been here for six months. He's not rehomeable. Too vicious. Savaged his owner, who ended up in hospital for weeks, for no apparent reason. Nobody's ever been in the kennel with him. Except me, that is.'

'Oh, thanks, Granddad. What if he'd attacked me? He might have killed me.' Olivia hadn't exactly been afraid. But she hadn't exactly felt confident either.

'I knew he wouldn't bite you. You don't show fear. If I'd told you what he was like before, he'd have sensed the fear. Then you'd have been in trouble. You're like your mum. She was fearless around the dogs too. Never ever got bitten. She was about your age when I started letting her help me feed them. She even did it a few times on her own. You're so alike, it's uncanny.'

Olivia pictured her mum feeding the dogs like she'd just done. She felt a stab in her heart, but she longed to know more and it wasn't often that Granddad would talk about Mum. 'She loved Kymera, didn't she, Granddad?'

'She did.' Granddad nodded. 'She always wanted to be here. Of course we didn't live here then. We lived in a proper house, believe it or not, her, me and Nick. But she spent as much time with me at Kymera as possible. She became a little strange, well, not strange exactly, more… dreamy, I suppose. She preferred being with the dogs than with people, especially after your grandmother came back. Pff!' Granddad shook his head at the memory.

'She had a special dog, didn't she?' Olivia leaned forward eagerly.

'That's right. Molly.'

'What happened to her? Molly?'

'She died eventually. Like we all do.' Granddad looked evasive as he stood up to put the kettle on. 'Anyway that's when your mum did all the paintings. She reckoned Molly inspired her.'

'Paintings? What paintings?'

There was a sudden commotion as a rat scurried across the kitchen floor from out of the bathroom and made a run for it out the door into the garden. Queenie, Queenie Two, Valentino and even Soldier went shooting after it, although it was more of an enthusiastic amble in Soldier's case. A high-pitched squeal signified that one of them had been quick enough to nab the poor thing. Seconds later, Queenie, looking very pleased with herself, appeared with it in her mouth.

'Queenie,' yelled Olivia, 'take it away. That's horrible.'

Queenie, looking offended, sloped off, followed by the other dogs.

'I'd best get it off her,' said Archie. 'I don't want her eating it, though I doubt that she would.'

'Wait, Granddad. You were telling me about the paintings.'

'The paintings, yes,' said Granddad. 'She painted all those strange creatures on the sign at the entrance to Kymera. You probably haven't noticed them. They're all faded now. People came from all over to see them. She was a very talented artist, you know. She used to say it made the place safe, conjured up the benevolent spirits to help keep evil out. She had a very vivid imagination, your mum. Mind you, we were doing pretty well then, not mega rich or anything like that, but definitely holding our own. She used to help me a lot, did my Jess. I wish…' Granddad's voice faded away. 'I'd best go sort Queenie out,' he said, clearing his throat and heading for the door.

Olivia suddenly had a vague flash of images on the Kymera sign. She recalled how she'd noticed them on her seventh birthday as they arrived, although they hadn't been hugely visible even then. With everything that happened that day, she'd not given them another thought and, it was true, she hadn't noticed them since. The purple dragon on the door of the treehouse had become barely discernible too. It would be her mission to bring them all back to life, carry on what Mum had started.

She went to rummage in her bedroom for the painting set Mum and Dad had given her one birthday, she couldn't remember which one. Had she brought it with her when she moved? She had only the haziest memory of the move itself and what she had and hadn't packed.

It turned up at the bottom of one of the cardboard boxes. Phew. That was a relief.

Queenie wandered into the bedroom, minus rat fortunately, and jumped up on to the bed next to Olivia, who was clutching the painting set to her. Queenie nodded her approval, or so it seemed to Olivia.

'You'd better not have eaten that rat, Queenie,' said Olivia. Queenie shook her head. 'D'you know what, Queenie? As soon as we've got that little pup eating properly and persuaded Granddad that she should stay…You want her to stay, don't you, Queenie?' Queenie nodded her head vigorously. 'As soon as we've got Granddad onside, I'm going to paint over whatever it was that Mum drew on the gate and make it look all nice and welcoming again. Or perhaps we'll sort out some of those dogs in the Big Kennels first. I might even take them for a walk on the Moors, get them used to going out and mixing more, then maybe we can find them their forever homes. After that, or before even, we'll spruce the place up. What d'you reckon, Queenie? Shall we start with making sure the little pup stays?'

Queenie wagged her stumpy tail, jumped off the bed and raced around the bedroom.

'I knew you'd agree with me. We've just got to convince Granddad that we know what's for the best. It's a plan.'

13. Back to Me, Me, Me

KAT

Hello again. I expect you're wanting to hear a little more about how I've been getting on in this new and rather alarming world I've landed in.

Well…the first couple of days passed in rather a blur, with my sisters not giving a jot whether I got to feed off Mum or not. In fact, I'd go as far as to say that they were doing their best to keep me out of the way, greedy lot. Sometimes Olivia or Archie would make a point of picking me up and attaching me to one of Mum's busts, which was bliss for a few short minutes. Then they'd go and do something else and I'd get shoved aside again.

When I was four days old, still recovering from the trauma of my birth, I was subjected to yet another totally terrifying experience.

Olivia and Archie were in the Puppy Palace talking about what I soon came to realize was a terrible act of violence against dogs. It's true that you shouldn't listen in to other people's conversations if you only want to hear nice things. Apparently, that's called eavesdropping. But I so love the sound of Olivia's voice, I couldn't help but tune in.

'Do we have to do this, Granddad?' she started off saying. 'I like them with tails. Nobody cuts them off anymore. It's not even fashionable. I mean, is it even legal?'

'LEGAL? Pff! I'm not having anybody dictating to *me* about dogs. What the heck do *they* know? People prefer them without tails, I'm telling you. In my day you never saw a Jack Russell with a tail. They simply don't look right.'

'That was donkey's years ago, Granddad. A lot of them have tails nowadays. Anyway, it's cruel. It's barbaric.'

'Barbaric, is it? Hark at you with your big words. Believe me, they don't even feel it. I've done hundreds in my time. A Jack Russell with a tail isn't a proper Jack Russell.'

Hmm. Ever wondered where we dogs might stand on this one, Archie?

'Ssh, Granddad. They might hear you.'

'Na, they can't hear anything at this age. Not that they'd understand even if they could.'

'I'm not so sure, Granddad. I think the little one understands what *I'm* saying.'

Of course I do, Olivia.

'Anyway, Valentino's got a tail.'

'Ah well, he was the one that got away, wasn't he? And he isn't the real deal. I'm pretty sure his dad was Old Soldier, which would make him half and half, half Jack Russell and half Cavalier King Charles. He was another one from a big litter, all boys that time if I remember right. We couldn't get shut of him. Nobody wanted him. That's why he ended up staying.'

'Ah, poor Valentino. I love Val.'

'Poor Valentino indeed. He's got the life of Riley, that lad.'

Then Archie sets off singing, not particularly tunefully I have to say, 'Slugs and snails and puppy dogs' tails, that's what little boys are made of.'

'Have you just made that up?' says Olivia. 'It's quite funny actually. What about little girls, like all of these?'

'Sugar and spice and all things nice and not a tail beee…tween them,' sings Archie. 'Right. How's about I practise on you first?'

I can hear a bit of a scuffle going on and Olivia screaming and laughing at the same time. 'Get off my hair, Granddad.'

'Oi,' I hear Archie say. 'You want to keep those pigtails in check. They're lethal.'

I'm sure you can imagine how I'm feeling by now. To give you a clue, I've eased my way round the back of Mum out of sight. And I'm proper shaking. My sisters just carry on suckling on Mum, in true 'dim dog' fashion, if you get my meaning. It's not their fault. I don't suppose they can help it if there's not a lot going on upstairs.

'Are they even sharp, those scissors?' says Olivia. 'They look old and blunt to me.'

What? Somebody help!

'I suppose they *have* seen better days. Let's test them out on one of your fingernails.'

I hear more laughing and scuffling, and then, 'Ow, Granddad! You see. You can't possibly use them. They're useless.'

'Hmm. We're just going to have to improvise. Looks like it'll have to be the old gnashers.'

I hear an ominous chattering sound.

'You're not serious, Granddad. Stop doing that. You look like that serial killer in *Silence of the Lambs*.'

'I'm no serial killer. But I can fancy the odd tail or two,' says Archie as a sucking sound joins the teeth-chattering.

'Stop it, Granddad.'

'Don't be so soft. Mrs Burton did them all like that for years and she's been breeding dogs since before you were born, probably since before *I* was born even.'

'Oh, and I suppose Mrs Burton licked up all their poo for them too, did she?' says Olivia.

'You can be a very nasty little girl at times, d'you know that? We'll have to change your name to Miss Nastyitis,' says Archie.

By now, I'm wishing myself back inside Mum's tum, even with all my squirming, kicking sisters. Anything's better than what I fear lies ahead. I wonder about making myself disappear. I've a feeling I should know how to do this because, to be honest, I do feel a bit special.

'You know what?' says Archie. 'I think my *teeth* have gone blunt now. You're going to have to do the dirty deed, Miss Nastyitis.'

'There is no way I'm biting off any dog's tail. Absolutely, definitely, categorically not.'

'Come on now, one quick bite. That's all it takes. Get those dainty little gnashers in action my girl. You'll never be a proper Dogwalla, not until you've bitten off a tail or two.'

There are more sucking and chattering noises, followed by a burst of laughter from Archie.

'For goodness' sake, Granddad. You never intended cutting their tails off, did you? And stop waving those scissors around like a demented serial tail-chopper-offer.'

'Just testing, just testing. I actually quite like them with tails.'

As you can tell, Archie fancies himself as a bit of a joker. Somebody ought to tell him that it's not funny scaring a little pup like that.

14. Dog Guardian

Duke

Duke was feeling better. His leg was nearly like new and Archie and Bob had decided between them that he should stay at Kymera. He was fond of Bob, but he'd always felt more at home at Kymera. He had been born there after all, so he was only going back to his roots. Besides everywhere else paled in comparison. Life outside Kymera was not exactly boring, just ordinary and dog-like. He was also secretly fond of the old queen, though he'd never admit it to her. And, with him visiting so often over the years, he'd got pally with Oberon, Kymera's resident horse. Queenie called him the nitwit nag. She thought she knew everything, but she wasn't as clever as she liked to think.

Going out with Olivia and Oberon was Duke's most favourite thing in the world - flying across the Moors, chasing bunnies, which he never caught (although of course he could have if he'd wanted). They made a proper good threesome. He loved watching Olivia as she brushed Oberon until his coat shone like polished ebony. She'd chatter away to him, Oberon nodding and snorting as if he understood her every word. You smell so good, she'd say, putting her arm around his neck and shutting her eyes as she pressed her nose into his jet-black mane. She'd often give him a handful of nuts as she worked and she always had some little round mints in her pocket, which Oberon would snuffle at to remind her. There you go, handsome, she'd say, slipping him a couple and dropping one or two on the floor for Duke. We like them, don't we, mate? Duke would remark and Oberon would whinny and nod his head, making Olivia laugh, even though she couldn't understand what they were saying. It made Duke's chest feel all warm and squishy watching them together.

When Olivia placed the saddle on Oberon's back and then shook out his bridle and put it over his head, Duke could barely contain his excitement. Shush, Duke, Olivia would say, you'll disturb the boarders and then Granddad will be cross.

Queenie sometimes stood by watching disapprovingly, feigning contempt of Duke's choice of companion and their 'gallivanting' as she called it, when really it was obvious that she was jealous of a horse.

The business at Bob's had unnerved Duke slightly. When he'd spotted those thugs hanging round the house with their horrible long, greasy hair, his first thought was that they were planning to rob Bob and his missus and he needed to be on his guard. Then he noticed one of them holding a net as they advanced tentatively towards him. A piece of meat landed at his feet and, as he bent his neck to inspect it, he felt himself grabbed from behind. Wheeling round, he'd struggled free and clamped his jaws around the bare arm of the grabber. Let go, you mangy mutt, he heard the man yell. Then there was a flash and a bang and his leg felt like it was on fire. Let's get out of here. With any luck, that'll finish him off, said another voice. We can report back, job done.

Next thing Duke knew, some foul-tasting stuff was being poured down his throat, which made him pass out, and he'd woken to find himself in the Puppy Palace.

***

Duke was not a pure breed, his parentage being somewhat in doubt. His mother was a fully-fledged Border Collie for sure, and he himself was convinced his father was pure Alsatian. Stocky in build, with not an ounce of fat on him, he was blessed with bright eyes and a black and white silky coat to die for (Duke's unbiased opinion). Possessed of a certain *je ne sais quoi,* which made him popular with the bitches, he favoured the exotic pooch, which Queenie mocked him for, no doubt out of jealousy. He suspected she harboured a long-nurtured, unrequited love for him, of which she had never given any actual indication. But a chap knows these things.

The dream he'd had, under the influence of whisky, about being sent to protect La Lupina, was starting to niggle him. He was trying hard to push it to the back of his mind, where he'd have very much liked it to stay. If only Queenie would keep her trap shut…

***

'You *do* know Doglore states that the dog who risks its life in an act of loyalty to its human is designated to be Dog Guardian, protector of La Lupina, don't you, Duke?' Queenie had come to visit Duke in the Puppy Palace, disturbing a nice little dream he was having about a glamourous, but rather tall, Afghan Hound called Grace. 'And this isn't the first time.'

'La, la, la, not listening, Queen. Although it was rather brave of me to stand my ground. I suppose that does make me a bit of a hero. But, to be truthful, I'm not convinced they were after robbing Bob. I think it was me they wanted to get their hands on.' Duke turned round a few times and pawed at his bed before settling into a cosy spot, only his head poking out from the rearranged jumpers.

'You?' said Queenie. 'What would they want with you?'

'Well, I'm a good-looking lad…'

'Piffle. Furthermore,' continued Queenie, undeterred, 'Doglore states that a dog shall be born with the ability to speak the human language from the moment of her birth…'

'So you're saying,' interrupted Duke, 'that this "chosen one", that mardy little runt that Olivia's always fawning over, can talk?'

'Indeed. She spoke to me from inside the womb.'

Duke raised his eyebrows. 'Oh aye. And what did she say to you from inside the womb?'

'She said, "Please don't leave me in here on my own. It's very dark. And I'm very tired."'

'Profound.'

'Well, how old were you before *you* could speak? I was twenty-one, in dog years of course, before I said *my* first words and I'm Top Dog of top dogs, Special amongst Specials, in total command, supreme ruler, queen of my domain, not just Kymera, but the whole of Dogsworld, elected by the Dog Council to…'

'Well, I've never heard the little rat utter a word,' interrupted Duke impatiently. 'How come you're the only one deluded enough to imagine you can hear it?'

'That, Duke, would be because I am Mrs Big, the superior, most powerful…'

Duke stifled a yawn. 'Yeah, yeah. I get the picture.'

'Face it, Duke. It's high time La Lupina made an appearance. Dim dogs are on the increase. Mixing with humans over the years has had a detrimental effect on the dog population. Humans like to think they're the superior race. But they're deluded. Take the human Top Dog - God. Humans think he's the cat's pyjamas.'

'The cat's pyjamas…? Why would they think that? I didn't know cats even *wore* pyjamas. What's wrong with a few old jumpers?' Duke burrowed further down into his self-made jumper bed.

'Just an expression, Duke. The cat's whiskers, if you like, or the bee's knees, or the dog's boll… no never mind. Humans think God is great. But God is simply Dog spelt backwards. God is Dog and Dog is God. Says it all. Dogs were here first. The human race is in for a long overdue kick up the backside.'

Queenie looked like the cat who'd got the cream, or rather the dog who'd got the bone. Sometimes she could be quite insufferable.

'You been watching too much telly?' said Duke. 'You don't want to believe everything you hear, you know, Queen. Anyway, this is getting boring.'

'Think of the numbers, then. Everything adds up. It's no coincidence.'

'Why now?'

'Because, Duke, my friend, Dogsworld is in deep trouble.' Queenie paused for effect. It was no use her looking at him like that. Duke was determined not to be drawn in. 'Dog theft is on the increase. Dogfights are springing up all over the place. The world is losing its soul. Evil is rampant.'

'Talk about drama queen, Queen. You've missed your calling. You should go on the stage.'

'You mark my words, Duke. Malina is out there somewhere, spreading her poison. La Lupina has been sent to put things right, to redress the balance. Let Good triumph over Evil!'

Queenie was really getting into her stride now. She'd be proclaiming it from the rooftops if Duke showed her the slightest encouragement. He yawned again, almost wishing he was back in the boring old normal world outside Kymera, where dogs just got taken for walks and had a nice dinner followed by a lovely snooze and there wasn't any talk of Lupinas, Malinas and certainly not reluctant Dog Guardians.

Almost, but not quite. He would never really want to be anywhere but Kymera.

15. Time For a Change?

'OY! I say! Where is everybody? Let's have a look at these 'ere pups then. Dad? Olivia?'

Oh no, Uncle Nick was here. Olivia stumbled out of her room, rubbing her eyes, hair all mussed up, nightie trailing on the floor. 'Granddad's in the Big Kennels, Uncle Nick, cleaning out the boarders. Have you come to see Katja?'

'Darn right I have, lass. I smell brass,' he said, laughing and rubbing his hands. 'Brass, lass. See what I did there? I'm a poet, me. Anyway, seven bitches, I hear. It's about time we had a bit of luck. I'll go take a peek. In the old Puppy Palace, are they?'

'Wait, wait, Uncle Nick. I'll come with you.' Olivia dashed into the bedroom and pulled on her jeans and pink 'I Love Horses' T-shirt. Stomach churning, she ran after him in her bare feet towards the Puppy Palace, shouting, 'Granddad, Granddad, Uncle Nick's here.'

Queenie and Valentino were right behind her, catching her up as Granddad emerged from the Big Kennels.

'He's come to look at the pups,' she whispered.

'Righto,' said Archie. 'I thought he'd be down

once he heard.'

He followed Uncle Nick into the Puppy Palace and slapped him on the shoulder. 'Hello, lad, nice to see you.'

'Dad?' said Uncle Nick, heaving his bulky form around.

They shook hands and patted each other on the arm.

'So these are the pups, eh?' said Uncle Nick, bending down to stroke Katja, who warned him off with a growl.

'Belt up, you, you little grump, don't you be getting nowty with me, or you'll know about it,' he said, straightening up and hitching his trousers round his fat belly. He looked thoughtful as he ran a hand through his thatch of oily black hair.

Olivia felt her blood run cold.

'I'll get you one to have a look at,' said Granddad, giving Katja a stroke and easing one of the pups off her teats. He held it out to Uncle Nick, who barely glanced at it before turning his attention to the others, squinting as he peered into the kennel.

Hide behind Katja, little one. Make yourself invisible.

'That one looks a bit puny,' he said, pointing straight at the little pup. 'What's up with it? Pass it here, Dad.'

Olivia held her breath, feeling the colour drain from her face, as Granddad picked the pup up and handed her over to Uncle Nick.

'Hmm,' he said, poking and prodding until she squeaked. 'Nowt special, but it'll do, I suppose. Some people like the runt. In fact I know somebody who's after a little'un.'

Olivia felt herself go even paler.

Another poke and prod…another squeak. 'So…? All bitches, eh, Dad? What are they? A week? Ten days?'

'Just over a week.'

'Another few weeks before we can get shut then. We can make a killing. Black and white, with a bit of tan on some of them. That'll do. I reckon they'll go for a good few hundred apiece, easy, a thousand if we're lucky. We've really landed on us feet for once.'

Archie frowned, but said nothing.

Olivia could feel her heart quickening and thudding. 'Shall *I* hold the pup, Uncle Nick?' she stammered.

'Why? What's it to you? Here, put it back in with the rest. Don't you be getting attached or owt. They'll be gone soon enough.'

'But… but, Granddad,' Olivia stuttered, clutching the pup, who licked her face and snuffled into her hair. 'We won't be selling all of them, will we, Granddad? What about…?'

'What about what, Olivia?' bellowed Uncle Nick. 'Of course we'll be selling all of them. What d'you think this is, a dogs' holiday camp?'

Olivia stared at Archie, who had found something interesting to look at in Katja's kennel.

'No room for sentiment in this game, lass,' said Uncle Nick. 'We need to make the most of these little bitches. Especially after the money we lost during the pandemic. I'm sorry, Olivia, but that's the way it is. Isn't that right, Dad?'

'We'll see, we'll see,' said Archie, rubbing his forehead.

'I thought I might keep one of them, Uncle Nick,' Olivia managed to whisper. 'This one maybe. She nearly died, you know.'

'Keep one?' roared Uncle Nick. 'Not on your life, my girl. You've got Katja here and that waste of space, Soldier, lolling around the joint, neither use nor ornament. And as for that dozy article Queenie Two, eating us out of house and home. Not to mention that clown Valentino. Although, to be fair, he's earned his keep for once. I'm assuming he *is* the dad.'

Snatching the pup off her, he practically threw her back in with Katja, who tried to take a chunk out of his hand.

Atta girl, Katja. Olivia's face flushed the colour

of her T-shirt as she clenched her fists. She was practically boiling over with rage. No *way* was he getting rid of her little pup.

'And what's that old sheepdog still doing here?' said Uncle Nick, pointing at Duke, who was glaring at him from the next kennel. 'I heard Bob had brought it down for you to fix, Dad. Got shot, didn't it? Isn't it time it went back home? Looks all right to me.'

'He's staying,' said Archie. 'He'll make a pretty good guard dog, I reckon. And Bob…'

'Guard dog? What d'you need a guard dog for? You've nowt worth pinching. People see you coming, Dad, that's your trouble. Anyway, I've been looking at the books. If we don't make a good bit of money soon, we're going to have to think about selling the place.'

Olivia stared open-mouthed at Granddad, whose face had darkened with anger.

'Over my dead body,' he said quietly.

'You need to face facts, Dad. We can't survive on fresh air. Maybe you should think about retiring. Time for a change. We could get a good price for the place.'

Granddad walked over to the boiler in the corner and began stirring the meat. 'I shall never retire, lad,' he said. 'This is my life. And my home. I don't much care for change.'

Olivia was on the point of bursting into tears. How could Uncle Nick be so horrid to poor Granddad?

'Just think about it, Dad. You'll see it makes sense. You could get a decent place for you and Olivia with your half.'

The smell of the tripe bubbling away in the corner was making Olivia feel nauseous. 'I like it here. I don't want to move.'

'It's not really up to you,' said Uncle Nick, turning to look at Olivia in a way that made her insides feel all liquidy. 'You'll do as you're told, young lady, if you know what's good for you.

'Anyway, Dad, to change the subject, I've got our Pookah in the car. Thought she could come and live down here for the time being. The wife doesn't want her at home anymore, what with the lads having moved out. You know what Janey's like - not really dog-friendly - and there's no one to take her for walks these days. I told Janey you wouldn't mind.

'There you go,' he said, turning to Olivia and patting her on the head with a smile that reminded her of a grinning gargoyle. 'If you're so keen on having another dog, you can adopt Pookah, or that mangy mutt, Duke.'

Olivia flinched involuntarily. He'd better watch out. If he carried on patting her like a dog, she'd bite him like a dog.

'There we go. The perfect solution. Now everybody's happy. Make sure you look after her, young Olivia, or you'll have *me* to answer to. I'll go fetch her from the car.'

And off he stomped, a man on a mission.

'Granddad…?'

'Leave it for now, love,' he said. 'There are ways of handling that lad of mine. Let's wait and see what happens. You never know. *You* go and get some shoes on before you catch your death.'

'Here you are,' said Uncle Nick, strolling back in, an odd-looking dog tucked under his arm.

Unsettling pink eyes studied them from a totally black face perched on a pure white body except for a black tail.

Olivia felt a blast of cold air rush though the Puppy Palace.

'Our Pookah'll soon make herself at home,' said Uncle Nick. 'She'll be ruling the roost in no time.'

'In her dreams,' said Queenie to Duke. 'But no good will come of this. You mark my words, Duke. That Pookah bitch is trouble with a capital T.'

16. The Pup Gets a Nasty Shock

KAT

It's me again, with a quick update. Still nameless. It's almost like I'm not expected to stick around. They couldn't be more wrong. I'm going nowhere.

Life was starting to get a touch boring now, if I'm honest. OK, there was nothing wrong with being around Mum, whenever the others let me get a look in that is, and being spoilt with extra milk by Olivia, mixed with something called 'vitamins', which is supposed to be good for me. But there had to be more to life than this. And I don't mean being poked and prodded by Old Nick, as Queenie calls him. I'm just glad he isn't a regular visitor.

Anyway, a couple of weeks or so after the glorious birth (that would be mine, of course), everything changed.

Archie and Olivia came into the Puppy Palace and stood talking outside our kennel.

'They'll be opening their eyes any day now,'

says Archie. 'Then you'll start to see their little personalities develop.'

Now that *did* sound exciting. I couldn't wait for *my* eyes to open so that my personality could start developing, not that I was sure what a personality was, but mine was bound to be better than my sisters'.

I was also dying to see what Olivia and Archie looked like, and Queenie and Duke. And Mum especially. Even my sisters, although I imagined them all to look pretty much the same. Not very interesting. Not as interesting as I was convinced *I* must look. That may sound a little show-offy, but it's not my fault I feel special and different.

'The runt's picked up a lot,' says Archie, 'but it's not out of the woods yet.'

The runt? What kind of talk is that?

'What d'you mean, Granddad?' says Olivia, sounding upset.

'Oh nothing, love, nothing. It's thanks to you giving it all that extra milk and vitamins that it's got *this* far.'

'*This* far?' repeats Olivia, picking me up and cuddling me close. 'Why? She's going to be all right, isn't she? She *is* still very small, I suppose. Do you think she's *too* small? You do, don't you, Granddad?'

'No, course not, love. It's doing very well. It's

still just a little behind the others, that's all.'

Don't you worry, Olivia. I'm sticking with you. I snuggle as close to her as I can.

Suddenly Olivia screeches, 'Look, those two have opened their eyes,' and I'm plonked back down next to Mum as Olivia picks up one of my sisters.

'Oh, Granddad, isn't she sweet? Look at those lovely little eyes,' she says in a rather silly voice.

One by one, my sisters start scurrying about, with Olivia squealing and clapping her hands.

*Why won't **my** eyes open?* I struggle and struggle, trying to force them to do my bidding. I can barely breathe with the effort. Why do I always have to be last at everything? I sit in the corner sulking. And then, suddenly, my eyes pop open. Just like that.

First I look at Mum. Love at first sight. My, what a kind face she has. Then I have a peek at my sisters. All exactly alike, black and white, some with a bit of brown on them. I knew it. All the same. No surprises there. Finally, I stare down at myself. Oh no! What has gone wrong? I look just like them too. Not different. Not special. Just another dog. I feel my face crumple. This is a disaster.

Next minute I'm being swept up into the air and I find myself looking deep into Olivia's eyes.

'And what's the matter with this gorgeous girl?' she says, a beautiful smile lighting up her face, every bit as lovely as I knew it would be. Something so powerful passes between us that nothing else seems to matter. We'll always have that bond of love. Together forever. Sounds soppy, I know, but it *is* a very special moment.

Then I hear a low grumbling sound. I glance at Archie, who has a kindly expression on his face. I like him immediately, with his cap pushed back showing only a few strands of hair. I'm surprised to see that he's no taller than Olivia. It's definitely not him making that noise. I look down at his feet. Ugh! It's a dog with pink eyes. She doesn't look anything like the rest of us, with her white body and black tail. She's staring straight at me, really giving me the evils. The grumble turns into a snarl and Archie taps her with his foot. 'Cut it out, Pookah,' he says, but the horrid thing barks angrily at me.

What have ***I*** *done? Nasty bitch.*

Archie gives her a harder tap with his foot and Pookah's pink eyes glow viciously as she barks even louder.

'Shut up, Pookah,' says Olivia and Pookah turns her gaze on her, venom and hatred spewing forth from her eyes. How dare she? *Don't you look at my Olivia like that.* I feel myself go rigid as my eyes burn into the vile creature.

Abruptly she stops her barking and cowers back into the corner. *That's shown **her**!*

'What happened there?' says Olivia, turning to look at me. 'Wow, your eyes,' she squeals. 'I've never seen eyes like it before. Look, Granddad.'

Archie turns in my direction. 'What d'you mean, Olivia? Most Jack Russells have brown eyes. What's so special about this one?'

'Oh,' says Olivia, looking at me again. 'I could have sworn they were bright green a moment ago. How weird.'

That's when I know for sure that I really actually *am* something special.

17. Who the Heck's Pookah?

POOKAH

'What's with the old hackles, Queen?' said Duke, who had graduated from the Puppy Palace to the main house - Ky Manor, as Archie liked to call it - and made himself right at home in his new home, like he'd never lived anywhere else. 'You look as mad as a frog.'

Queenie didn't deign to reply. Duke could be very stupid at times. Both he and Archie were in her bad books. Pookah had taken up residence in the kitchen. Queenie did not approve. At all.

Queenie could remember Pookah as a pup. She'd been abandoned at the entrance to Kymera one dark night. The pup with the peculiar pink eyes had snarled at her straight off and she'd been snarling ever since. Her strange appearance appealed to Nick, as did her sour nature, which mirrored his own, so he decided to take her home for his two sons, Laurence and Felix. They'd always wanted a dog and were happy with their weird-looking snapdragon. Wherever the lads went, she followed them.

But it wasn't right, Nick dumping her on them like that. Only the select few made it to the Manor. Nobody had run it past Queenie first. Pookah had no right to join their little family. Why now? There had to be more to it.

'I smell a rat, Duke,' said Queenie. 'That bitch ain't right. I wonder if she's working for the enemy.'

'You been on the beer again, old girl?' said Duke, taking a chance on being turned into tomorrow's dinner.

'You'll see, Duke. I'm not queen for nothing. The old snitch has never let me down yet. And that bitch is a rat.'

'Stick a protective circle round the place if you're worried. Do your magic powers stretch that far, Queen?'

'Of course they do,' snapped Queenie. 'Hang on while I think of a spell.'

Queenie wrinkled her forehead as she searched for the words. This spell-casting business was hard work when she was so out of practice. 'Right, got it,' she said finally. 'Come outside with me, Duke. It might work better with two of us.'

Duke yawned, but followed her out anyway as she headed for the back field. Standing in front of the old willow tree, Queenie instructed Duke to stand opposite her, so that their front paws were touching. 'It'll strengthen the spell,' she explained.

'Right-oh, Queen, whatever you say.'

Queenie closed her eyes, twitched her tail and began to chant.

'I call upon the powers on high,
'To shield and free our precious Ky,
'From the presence of the Evil One,
'Malina! From our home be gone!'

'Blimey. A bit dramatic that, Queen,' said Duke. 'I'd definitely be clearing off if I was her.'

There was flash of lightening and a rush of wind through the branches of the old willow. Then nothing. Silence.

As they arrived back in the kitchen, Archie was attempting to feed the pup some warm milk from a bottle. 'Come on, open up,' he said, squeezing the sides of her mouth, trying to force the teat in.

No dog likes that kind of treatment and the pup was keeping her mouth stubbornly closed so that the milk was dribbling down on to her chest.

'Oi, stop that. It's horrible,' said a little voice.

Queenie's ears shot up. 'Can you hear me, Lupina? This is your great grandmother speaking.'

'Lupina…? You talking to yourself now,

Queen?' said Duke, flinging himself down on the once pink, now dirty brown, rug in front of the cooker and stretching full length.

'Didn't you hear it? Didn't you hear the pup, Duke?' Queenie poked him with her paw.

'Not a dicky bird. You're imagining it, Queen.'

'I'm telling you, Duke,' said Queenie. 'It's true. Remember, I *am* on a higher vibration than you. You've got to admit I *do* have the superior powers. I mean, you saw how I dealt with the Evil One just now.'

'What? Because it got a bit windy, you mean? Come on, Queen. It was a great little ditty, but…'

'Disbeliever,' yapped Queenie. 'I've a good mind…'

'Quit sniping at each other, you two,' said Archie. He turned towards Olivia. 'D'you want to have a go, love? The pup takes the milk better from you. It *is* suckling better, but it's still lagging behind the others.'

Snuggling down into the threadbare old chair, Olivia cuddled the pup like a baby, gently placing the teat between its lips. 'Come on, gorgeous, drink your milk. It'll make you big and strong.'

'Well, seeing as it's you,' said the pup, sucking greedily. 'Hmm, it's actually rather nice.'

'You see that, disbeliever?' said Queenie. 'The pup's talking to Olivia. She may not be able to hear us, but she can hear Olivia.'

'And *I'm* the King of the Wolves,' said Duke. 'NOT!'

'Belt up, you old cynic. I don't think Olivia can hear the pup though. She's not responded at all. Shame. Still, I think it's lovely how we all look out for each other,' said Queenie, suddenly feeling all warm and fuzzy inside.

'You having a maudlin moment, Queen?'

'Only saying. We've always been like one big happy family here.'

That's when Queenie's words came back to bite her. One minute she's wallowing in soppiness, off her guard, and the next that Pookah's flying through the air, snapping and snarling, pink eyes blazing.

Whoa. Where did *she* come from?

Teeth bared like a baby crocodile, Pookah landed on top of Olivia, knocking the bottle from the pup's lips as she tried to grab the little mite.

Olivia leapt up, clutching the pup, and threw Pookah to the floor.

Archie started yelling and aimed his boot at her, but Pookah dodged out of the way.

Duke rushed to stand guard over Olivia and the pup.

Valentino looked stunned.

Queenie Two carried on chomping on a stale

biscuit in true dim dog fashion.

Soldier stayed asleep behind the cooker.

Queenie went for the jugular. Well, not quite. But she gave that Pookah a nip she wouldn't forget in a hurry, causing the bitch to slink back to her corner, eyes glowing darkly red and menacing.

'That was close,' said Duke, when things had settled back down again. 'I have to say your spell doesn't seem to have been a total success, Queen. You losing your touch?'

'It's not a magic cure-all.'

'No? I thought that was exactly what it was supposed to be.' Duke raised his eyebrows.

'Shut up, Duke. You know what I mean. It just helps, that's all. It helps keep Malina out, but it doesn't stop her channelling a dog already on the place.' She jerked her head in the direction of Pookah, who was glaring at her from the corner of the kitchen.

'I'm not sure about the channelling business. I reckon you're making it up as you go along. But I'm prepared to admit that you could be right about that one. A proper nasty piece of work.'

'Hallelujah! What did I tell you? Where did the bitch come from to start with? We know it wasn't from here.'

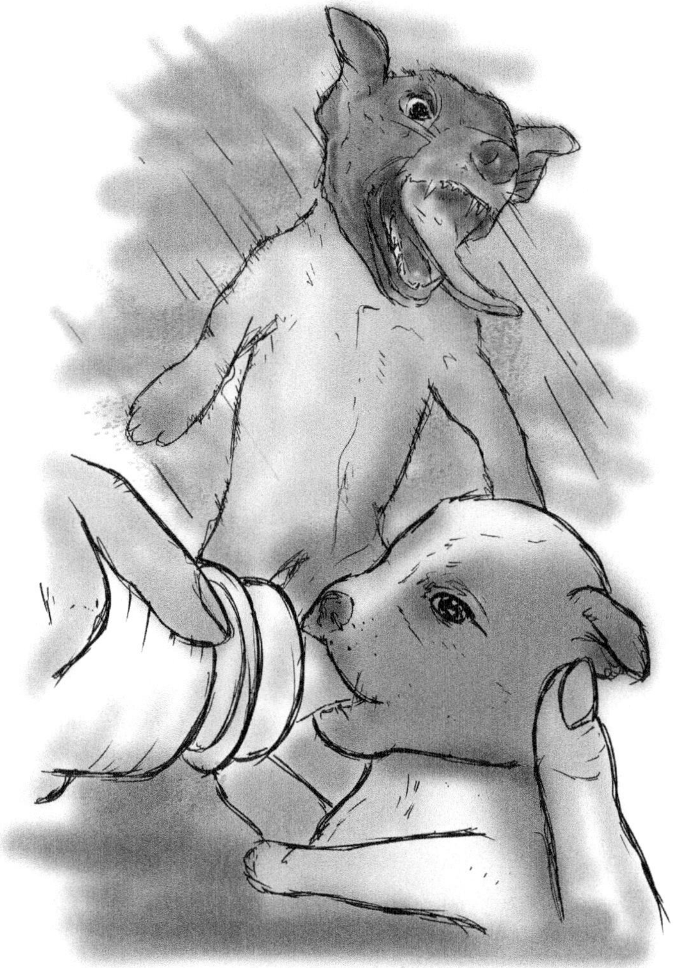

'What you saying, Queen?'

'I'm saying…'

'Not…' Duke arched his eyebrows.

'Not *her*, no, not Malina. Pookah's no match for me. Maybe one of Malina's Henchbitches, possibly even her Head Henchbitch. I'll bet my smelliest bone she's part of the Evil Alliance.'

18. Pandemics and Stuff

'Evil Alliance…? Give us a break, Queen.'

But Queenie was not one to be put easily off her stride. 'The world is inviting the Dog Antichrist to add her own brand of evil to the ills taking over the planet, Duke.'

'What does that even *mean*?' Duke shook his head. 'You're talking a load of twaddle, Queen. Evil Alliance? Ills? What ills? I just hope Olivia hasn't forgotten we're supposed to be going out with Oberon today.'

Queenie felt her coat bristling. Sometimes Duke managed a more than passable imitation of one of the dim dogs. 'If you weren't so wrapped up in yourself, Duke, you'd notice that the world is going all wrong, what with dog thefts, fighting, wars, and the pandemic. It's a window of opportunity for La Malina.'

'Really? And what's this pandemic when it's at home?'

Queenie could barely believe her ears. 'Where've you been hiding, Duke? You must remember the pandemic. It wasn't *that* long ago. People went around coughing all the time and lots died. It was horrid, especially when they died on their own, young and old. And it's not over yet. Archie got really upset about it. He called it a "global tragedy". I'm not sure what that means, but I'm pretty sure it's something very bad. He was ranting about the human race, politicians and pestilence and the four horses of the apocalypse…'

'Nowt wrong with horses, Queen, and, for your information, they have lovely soft lips. Talking of horses, Oberon's going to be getting impatient. I should go and see what he's up to.' Duke heaved himself to his feet and padded towards the kitchen door.

'What?' snapped Queenie. 'Not horses. I meant horsemen. I don't know about their lips, but there's plenty wrong with those horsemen, according to Archie. The end of the world as we know it. A perfect time for Malina to wangle her way into hearts and minds and create further havoc.'

'Right,' said Duke, stifling a yawn as he edged further towards the door.

'Come back here when I'm talking to you, you waste of space.' It wasn't often that Queenie allowed herself to get so worked up. 'People suffered terribly from loneliness. Some even bought dogs for company during the pandemic and then abandoned them when things got back to normal. It's lucky Archie had me for company or he might have gone completely doolally. I believe a lot of people did. That's how bad it was.'

'Yes, Archie's a very lucky man,' said Duke, attempting to sidle out the door.

'Surely you remember everybody going round with silly things over their faces, probably so they wouldn't be recognized and could get away with stuff.' Queenie nodded like she'd seen Archie do when he wasn't entirely sure about something. 'Even *Archie* covered his face when he went shopping, although everybody knew it was him. He looked a right pillock. I didn't like to be seen out with him. Then everybody stopped coming down here. Even *we* didn't see each other for ages.'

'That's right, Queen. I quite missed you.'

'Really?'

'No, I was joking.'

Queenie bared her teeth at Duke, who had made it to the top of the steps leading down to the garden. She briefly contemplated giving him a good bite, but then thought better of it. 'And that's why Archie's had all these money troubles, one of the reasons anyway. People stopped boarding their dogs and lots of abandoned dogs ended up at Kymera. More mouths to feed. You know Archie won't turn anyone away, not even ex-fighter dogs. Old Nick went on at him to "stop being a mug and let someone else look after the stupid mutts". He kept going on about grants, whatever they are, but Archie said he wasn't "taking no handouts from the government". They had terrific rows about it.'

'Nowt new there,' said Duke, moving in slow motion down the steps.

'At least the pups will bring in some cash when they're sold. Let's hope Malina doesn't get to those pups first though. She's bound to be after Lupina especially. Olivia will be able to persuade Archie to let her stay, I'm pretty sure of that. Lucky you're here to keep her safe. Maybe that was the reason you got attacked by those thugs, Duke, to try and prevent you taking up your role as Dog Guardian?'

'Maybe,' said Duke. 'Or maybe they just liked the look of a handsome chap like myself.'

Queenie snorted like a pig and turned her back on the self-deluded ignoramus, who was already legging it to the back field as she glanced over her shoulder.

My Seventh Birthday

Back in the garden, you and Dad were sitting at the rickety old table, holding hands across it, deep in conversation. You looked so happy, Mum. You both did.

The dovecote stood tall at the back of the table and a group of pure white doves were perched, chattering away to one another, like they were having a good old gossip. A couple of red-faced ducks, old Turner and Hooch, wobbled out of the lily pond and began parading around like King and Queen, flashing their bright lavender feathers and occasionally hissing grumpily and shaking their tails at any dog who ventured too close. Flowers of every imaginable variety, shape and size were in bloom everywhere I looked, in a dazzling array of colours. There were purples and yellows, reds and blues, golds and silvers, little pansies with their smiley faces next to tall ones I'd never seen before, colourful heads on thin stalks, all craning up, fighting to be noticed, or swaying from side to side in the gentle breeze.

I wandered over to the greenhouse, directly behind the dovecote, and peered through the glass. It was jammed full of the reddest tomatoes and brownest eggs I'd ever seen.

'Come and sit here, love,' you said, patting the seat next to you. 'Granddad's got a surprise for you.'

'I love it here, Mum. Can we come again soon? Please, oh please say yes,' I begged.

You gave a strange kind of smile. 'I hope so, darling. I've really missed the old place.'

I wonder. Did you know then what Fate had in store for us all?

19. Canine Communication

Queenie and Duke were watching Olivia fondly as she fussed and chattered to the pup during one of her daily feeds although, now she was nearly four weeks old, she probably could have managed without the extras. 'I think Granddad might have money problems,' she whispered to her. 'I'm still going to try and persuade him to let you stay though. I know he'll have to sell the others. We can't keep all the pups, much as I'd like to.'

'No, no. We don't need them,' said the pup.

Archie, who was making a cuppa for himself and Olivia (and hopefully Queenie), looked over. 'Are you talking to yourself? Or are you talking to that pup?'

Olivia laughed.

'She's talking to me of course,' said the pup

Queenie threw a significant look Duke's way.

'What? What now?' said Duke, stretching and yawning. 'Stop keep looking at me like that.'

'I haven't seriously studied Doglore since I was preparing for my quizzing from the Dog Council to sanction my election as Top Dog,' said Queenie. 'But you, for some reason, are pretty clued up in that department.'

'That would be my fantastic memory, Queen. I wasn't called *The Memory Dog* for nothing.' Duke looked smug. 'Why? What d'you want to know about Doglore?'

'What does it say about canine communication?'

'Canine communication? Dogs talking, you mean? Why don't you just say that? You hearing voices again, Queen? They can put you away for that, you know.' Duke wandered over to Olivia and gazed up at her as if willing her to take Oberon out for a jaunt.

'Yes, I *am* hearing voices, *one* voice in particular, to be exact, La Lupina's voice to be exactly exact.'

'Oh no, here we go again.' Duke sloped back to face Queenie, not having made much progress with Olivia, whose entire attention was focused on the pup. 'How many times, Queen? It's all in your mind. You *want* it to be true. Just forget about all that Lupina nonsense.'

'How many times, Duke? It isn't in my mind. Remember, I'm the Special of Specials, Top Dog, Queen Bee…'

'You can say that again,' interrupted Duke. 'And we all know what the 'B' stands for.'

'… which is why *I* can hear her, of course,'

continued Queenie, ignoring the numbskull. 'But why can't *you*? I mean you *are* capable of communication, on a good day. And why can't she hear *me*? I know it's in Doglore somewhere. The key that unlocks the power… What is it, Duke? Come on, Doglore expert.'

Duke likes a challenge. His eyes glazed over and he suddenly drew himself up to his full height and began to chant in a monotone, like he was being channelled by a zombie dog:

'The gift of understanding
'Is given to the few
'And granted only on the day
'That some will come to rue.'

'Well remembered, Duke. Though I'm not so sure about the "rue" part,' said Queenie. 'For a sheepdog-cum-bulldog, you have your uses. But lose the voice, it's creepy.'

'Sheepdog-cum-Alsatian with a brain sharp enough to slice through the toughest bone, if you don't mind,' said Duke in his normal voice. 'But what does it mean?'

'I think it means that one day, say the day you actually *catch* a rabbit – that would make a change, wouldn't it? - you too will hear La Lupina speak.'

'No! You mean I'm destined to hear what the little rat has to say for itself? Wow, I can't wait for that day to come.' Duke stretched his lips back in what could almost pass for a smile.

'I knew you'd come round to my way of thinking, Duke.'

'Never heard of sarcasm, Queen? *Can* actually wait, hopefully a very long time. Anyway, I don't see why Olivia has to slobber over the runt like that,' said Duke, looking glum.

'You're going to have to share, old lad. It's in a good cause. Remember your dream about being the pup's guardian and designated protector of La Lupina. She's going to need our help in the fight against La Malina.' Queenie nodded wisely.

'There you go again, Queen.' said Duke. 'You aren't half letting your imagination run away with you these days.'

20. Duke's Story

Duke

Queenie was having a serious think in the kitchen, when Olivia and Duke burst in, fresh from an outing with Oberon.

Olivia threw herself down on the scruffy old armchair and was immediately dog-mobbed.

'Fancy a cuppa, love?' said Archie, who had been washing up a few pots at the kitchen sink.

'That would be great, Granddad, thanks. I'm parched,' she gasped.

'Me too,' said Queenie.

'You're a proper teaholic, you,' said Duke, who preferred a nice bowl of water.

'Stop it. I can't breathe,' said Olivia, only her head visible under a pile of dogs, all competing to lick her to death.

'BEHAVE, YOU BRAINLESS NITS,' shouted Archie to zero effect, as Olivia continued to look like she was about to drown under a sea of tongues and tails.

'Some decorum, please, you lot,' barked

Queenie. The dogs looked warily at each other before settling on and around Olivia.

'Queenie's so good at handling the dogs. You could learn a few things from her, Granddad,' said Olivia, breathing a sigh of relief.

'Aye, she's a knowing dog is our Queenie,' said Archie. 'She's…'

'Yes, we all know, Granddad. She's a grand little dog.'

'She's my special little dog, not another like her.'

Queenie did a dog smirk for Duke's benefit, who did his best to look bored by the whole business.

'Duke's special too though, isn't he, Granddad?'

Duke perked up and did his own dog smirk at Queenie, who looked straight through him.

'Oh aye. He's a good lad is our Duke. Always the same – an honest, faithful fella, a bit like myself. Wouldn't you agree?'

'Absolutely, Granddad. Tell us the story of how Duke saved that man's life.' Olivia took a sip of her tea. 'Go on.'

'Old Billy, you mean?' said Archie, as if he didn't know perfectly well who Olivia was talking about. 'You've heard that story loads of times.'

'Yes, I know, but I want to hear it again.'

'All right then, I suppose it is a good story.'

'It's a *great* story,' said Duke, nudging Queenie with his nose.

'It's an all-right story,' said Queenie. Nowhere near as interesting as *her* story, and it was ages since Archie had told *that* one.

'Are we sitting comfortably?' said Archie.

Olivia nodded. Queenie shook her head.

'Then I'll begin. So…Billy, Billy Whitehead he was called, you won't remember him, Olivia, way before your time. He lived in that ramshackle farm at Potter's Brook. I gave Duke to Billy when he was just a pup, in exchange for some bales of hay. He'd taken a real fancy to him and Duke went home with him quite happily. He didn't have a life of luxury because Billy believed dogs should sleep outside and earn their keep.'

'Ah, poor Duke. I'm sure he's glad he's back here with us now.' Olivia gave him a pat. Queenie turned her back.

'They rubbed along, the two of them, old Billy and Duke. Anyway, rumour had it that Billy had some valuable jewellery, supposed to have been left to him by his mother, old Ma Whitehead. Billy never married, you know, lived with his mam until the day she died.

'There was a break-in at the farm, a couple of young lads, by all accounts. They'd got hold of an old rifle from somewhere. I don't think they really meant to use it, but Billy came back from wherever he'd been and surprised them. They threatened him with the gun and young Duke – he was only about six months old then – sprang to Billy's defence. The gun went off and Duke got caught in the crossfire. Shot in the leg, he was. The lads scarpered, but I believe they caught up with them eventually.'

'Ahem. Tea…?' said Queenie.

'Ssh, Queenie. I love this next bit.' Duke was gazing at Archie with a soppy look in his eyes.

'So what happened to Duke, Granddad?'

'Well, Billy brought him here. A right state he was in, poor Duke – unconscious, in shock and he'd lost a lot of blood. Old Billy said to me, "I reckon he's a goner, Archie, but if anybody can save him, *you* can." So I took care of him, night and day, dressing his wound, feeding him from a dropper. Brought him back to life, I did.'

'When you've quite finished bigging yourself up, you might want to give a thought to those of us suffering tea deprivation,' said Queenie crossly.

Archie paused briefly to bend down and give Queenie a quick stroke.

'Quiet, Queen, you're only jealous,' said Duke. 'Go on, Archie. Carry on.'

'Aye, by that time, old Billy had got hisself

another guard dog – an Alsatian, hard as blooming nails, it was – so he said to keep Duke, since he'd come from here originally.'

'And after Duke had saved his life too.'

'Country folk are a strange breed, Olivia,' said Archie, getting up to put the kettle on. 'They're not like other folk. Animals are there for a purpose, and Billy needed a guard dog. Duke stopped here for a while, and then Bob took a shine to him, so I said he could take him home, provided he brought him back regularly to visit, particularly our Queenie. They'd grown quite close, you know.'

'Nonsense,' said Queenie with a determined shake of her head.

'Get away, Queen. You know it's true. Anyway, it's a great story, isn't it? I'm such a hero. Love it,' said Duke with a sigh.

'It's strange that should happen twice, isn't it, Granddad? I mean Duke getting shot. Was it the same leg?'

'D'you know, I think it was, Olivia. He's quite the survivor, our Duke, isn't he? Now you come to mention it, it does seem rather a coincidence that he should land up here twice after getting shot.' Archie poured out two cups of tea and handed one to Olivia.

'Where's mine?' barked Queenie.

'Not likely to forget *you*, am I, Queenie?' said Archie, pouring some tea into her bowl and adding some cold water from the tap so that she wouldn't burn her mouth.

Queenie lapped it up eagerly.

'Anyway, I need to be getting those dogs fed. You want to give me a hand, love?'

'Oh yes,' said Olivia, leaping up and scattering the dim dogs all around the floor. 'I need to look at Katja and my little pup too. I haven't seen them since I got back.'

***

'You know what, Duke? Olivia's right. It *is* odd. Once you'd recovered from the trauma of nearly dying that first time was when you started to talk. It was like something was released in you.'

'I think you're reading too much into it, Queen,' said Duke, yawning and stretching. 'I was always a bright lad.'

'Yes, but it was only here at Kymera that you found your voice. You started quoting Doglore at me. Remember?'

'Found my voice? Who d'you think I am? The little mermaid?'

'No, I think you're the Dog Guardian to La Lupina. You've returned to fulfil your destiny,

Duke. Two acts of bravery.' ('Or stupidity,' she muttered under her breath.)

'I heard that, Queen. Destiny, my arse. Sorry, bottom. All that tea's going to your head. There's nowt wrong with a nice dish of water. You should try it some time.'

21. Night Time Shenanigans

Olivia was fast asleep. Valentino had crept on to the bed and was lying next to her. He'd squeezed himself between her and the pillow she was always clutching. Her arm was draped over him and they were breathing in time with each other.

Duke was on the floor at the foot of the bed. He'd have liked to be on the bed too, if only he would fit. Not that he hadn't attempted it but, being a well-built lad, he tended to end up pinning Olivia's legs down. And nobody likes that. Inevitably, Olivia, in the grip of one of her nightmares, would give a violent jerk of her squashed limbs, sending the poor boy flying. So he was inclined to stick to the floor, where he could dream uninterruptedly of lamb bones and fish, two things he was extremely fond of. Racing over the fields with Oberon also featured prominently in his dreams. Those twitching feet were a dead giveaway.

***

On the night in question, Queenie was sleeping in the bed with Archie next door as usual when she was woken by a noise. She turned around and around on her special feather cushion next to Archie's pillow. Still she couldn't settle, so she slithered quietly off the bed so as not to wake Archie. He was snoring away as per, with his crystal-clear conscience.

Queenie nudged open the bedroom door to see Duke padding out of Olivia's bedroom. Duke could always be relied on to sniff out trouble. His snitch was second only to Queenie's.

They looked at each other and then round the kitchen. *Oh-oh … no Pookah*, they both realized at the same time. And the kitchen door was half open.

A faint, high-pitched barking was coming from the direction of the Puppy Palace.

'Quick, Duke,' said Queenie.

The two of them shot over there at full pelt.

As they hurtled into the Puppy Palace, they skittered to an abrupt halt, horrified at the scene of carnage unfolding before them.

Pookah had somehow managed to scale the sides of the pen and was inside with Katja and her pups. She had Katja cornered and the two of them were snapping and snarling at each other. Katja was doing her best to defend herself. But she was no fighter. Pinned up against the back wall, she glanced over at the pups, who were cowering in the corner, terrified and whining. The little pup was lying to one side, not moving, as blood seeped from one of her ears.

Queenie and Duke leapt up at the bars of the kennel at the same time. Pookah glanced over and then pounced on Katja, turning her upside down. She was like a mad dog, eyes red like the devil's. Saliva dripped from her gnashing jaws as she tore into Katja.

Katja squealed loudly in pain and fear.

Pookah saw her chance and clamped her jaws around Katja's throat.

The pups were now yelping and howling as they watched their mother struggling for her life. Only the baby lay there, seemingly devoid of life.

The noise was deafening.

Blood and fur were flying everywhere.

Queenie, still foggy from sleep, couldn't for the life of her conjure up a single magic spell that might put a stop to the horrific attack and save Katja and the pup's lives. She braced herself and jumped up at the bars again, but it was no good. She was too small to get past halfway. 'Do something, Duke,' she barked frantically.

Duke made a giant leap and got his front paws over the top, scrabbling at the bars with his back legs in an attempt to launch himself over. Queenie jumped up again and head-butted his legs, so that he hurtled up and into the pen, landing awkwardly on top of Katja and Pookah, who separated. Duke shouted at Pookah to back off. She moved away, snarling. Nobody is brave or foolish enough to take on an angry Duke. He struggled to his feet and stood between the two bared-teeth opponents.

Katja hobbled slowly over to the pup, who lay comatose, blood oozing out into the sawdust on the floor, and began nuzzling the little body.

Queenie needed to act. Time was running out.

Archie would know what to do.

***

She practically flew back to the Manor and leapt on top of Archie, who sat up with a start, hair sticking out like a porcupine's quills. 'Emergency. Emergency. Get your backside to the Puppy Palace. NOW.'

Archie blinked sleepily at her.

'Move it, man,' she yelled.

Olivia appeared at the door, in her several-sizes-too-big winceyette nightie, rubbing her eyes. 'What's going on, Granddad? What's up with Queenie?'

Valentino was behind her, stretching and

yawning.

Queenie leapt off the bed barking and made for the kitchen door.

Archie sprang into action, grabbing an old coat to put over his pyjamas and throwing a manky old dressing gown at Olivia. He yelled at her to get some shoes on as she padded barefoot after Queenie.

She grabbed an old pair of Archie's shoes, which were lying around in the kitchen.

Archie made do with his not-so-new slippers.

They made a comical picture, shuffling along after Queenie in their ill-fitting footwear.

Only there was nothing funny about *this* situation.

Valentino ambled along behind.

Queenie Two stayed snuffling round the kitchen looking for food. Typical. No head for a crisis.

***

Olivia gasped in horror when they got to the Puppy Palace to find Katja, covered in blood, standing over the little pup. 'What's happened? Do something, Granddad,' she wailed, grabbing Archie's arm.

Archie shook her off, unbolted the door and

strode in, ordering Pookah and Duke out.

Horrid, evil Pookah slunk off.

Duke stood his ground.

Archie pushed him out of the way and bent down to where Katja was frantically licking the little pup. He gently eased her aside and picked up the limp little body.

'Please don't let the pup die,' sobbed Olivia. 'Please help her, Granddad.'

Come on, Archie. You saved the pup's life once. You can do it again.

22. Miracles Can Happen

'She's not dead, is she, Granddad? Please say she's not dead.'

Archie, sitting on the old armchair in the kitchen, with the little pup on his knee, wrapped in a blanket, momentarily paused his massaging of the pup's heart with his thumb. He looked down at Olivia, who was crouched on the floor, bathing Katja's wounds in a washing-up bowl. 'No, it's not dead, but it's not coming round either,' he said, resuming his massaging.

'She will do though, won't she, Granddad?'

'I don't know, Olivia. Things happen with livestock. That's the way it is. We'll give it a fighting chance though. It's all we can do.'

'And poor Katja…' The water, laced with disinfectant Olivia had found in the bathroom cupboard, was stained red with blood. 'She doesn't seem to be badly hurt though. I think it's mainly surface wounds.'

Katja gazed up at her, a grateful look in her eyes, as Olivia gently dried her off with a towel from the bathroom. Then she glanced over towards the pup and gave a feeble bark as if saying, Never mind me, save the pup.

'I'll warm up some milk and put a drop of brandy in it,' said Archie. 'Maybe make the little mite a hot water bottle too.'

As he got up to pour some milk into a pan and turn on the cooker, he handed the pup to Olivia. 'Here, *you* try. It's maybe in shock.'

Olivia sat herself down in the chair and began to copy what Granddad had been doing, gently massaging the pup's heart and, now and then, holding the pup to her ear to see if she could hear a heartbeat.

The pup remained limp and comatose.

Queenie and Duke came to sit at her feet, gazing anxiously up at her.

'Come on, I know you're in there,' muttered Archie, as he scrabbled around at the back of the kitchen cupboard in search of the extremely old bottle of cooking brandy, which hadn't seen daylight for years. 'There you are,' he said, dragging it out and pouring a big dollop into the hot milk. Waiting for it to cool down, he put the kettle on to boil, one of the old-fashioned types that sit on top of the hob and make a loud whistling noise when they're ready.

Olivia was feeling like she might spontaneously combust at any moment as she watched him pour the warm milk and brandy into a feeding bottle. 'Hurry up, Granddad. I don't think she's breathing.' *Please, God, don't let my little pup die.*

'There we go,' said Archie, handing her the bottle. 'Try it with this. If it won't take it, put a drop on its lips.'

Olivia gently prised the pup's mouth open, placed the teat inside and gave the bottle a squeeze. A few drops dribbled out of the side of her mouth. *Oh God, just drink some, please.*

Suddenly Queenie started leaping up at her and nudging the pup with her nose.

'Get off, Queenie.' Olivia pushed her away. 'We're trying to save baby's life.'

Queenie started to bark, followed by Duke, then Valentino and Queenie Two. The place was in an uproar. Even Old Soldier was doing his bit from behind the cooker.

'PACK IT IN,' yelled Archie. 'See to them, Queenie.'

The dogs took no notice. If anything, the barking increased in volume, with Queenie throwing in the odd howl for good measure. Duke seized hold of the old dressing gown Olivia had draped round her and started tugging.

'GET OFF, DUKE.'

'I think we should maybe leave things to Queenie,' said Archie. 'She'd never hurt it and maybe she knows something *we* don't. See what she wants with it. She's a smart little dog, our Queenie. It might be its only chance.'

Duke let go of Archie's dressing gown as Olivia gently laid the pup on the floor next to Queenie.

Valentino and Queenie Two stopped their barking.

Only Old Soldier carried on, the lone barker.

'Oh, do shut up, Soldier,' said Archie.

Soldier snuffled and flopped down in a heap.

The whole place fell into silence.

All eyes were on Queenie, who took a few long deep breaths.

As she stood over the pup, in a trance-like state, not a sound could be heard.

The room began to shimmer, as if a snowstorm had found its way into the kitchen. Olivia felt a rush of energy being harnessed from somewhere not of this world. Her breathing slowed right down and her arms and legs felt heavy like lead. She couldn't even blink and yet all of her senses were on high alert.

She heard Queenie growling rhythmically as she waggled her tail. Then she gave the pup three slow licks from head to toe, staggered away and collapsed on the floor.

The pup's eyelids started to flutter. She gave a long sigh, sat up and looked all around as Queenie got to her feet and gave herself a good shake.

'What the blimey heck happened there?' said Archie, sounding dazed, as though awakening from a deep sleep.

'It's a miracle, Granddad. Queenie just performed a miracle. It was almost like she was chanting a magic spell. Did you not hear her?' Olivia's fingers and toes were coming back to life and her breathing began to quicken up. She bent down to pick up the pup, who licked her nose. *Thank you, God.* 'You're all right, baby. Queenie's saved your life. She's a miracle worker.'

'No such things as miracles. And as for magic spells…' Archie laughed. 'It was mighty strange that though. Never seen anything like it in all my years. Perhaps it was the brandy that did it.'

'But she didn't really get any of it.'

'No, that's true,' said Archie, taking the bottle off Olivia, removing the teat and downing the lot.

'Granddad! The pup might want some more of that.'

'Hmm. I don't think so. Looks as right as rain to me. And we can't be letting good brandy go to waste now, can we? Not the price it is …'

23. The Past is a Different Universe

Olivia was in the kitchen, Ellie Goulding blasting out from her phone, as she sang along to *How Long Will I Love You*, when Granddad poked his head round the kitchen door. Olivia immediately stopped singing, fully expecting him to say, *Turn that blooomin' racket off*, like he normally did. But instead he said, 'Don't stop singing, love. You sound just like your mother. She'd a beautiful voice. And so have you.'

'Ah, thanks, Granddad. It was one of her favourites, you know. She used to sing this one to me all the time. That's why I like it.'

'Ah,' said Granddad.

Once the track had finished the two of them sat in silence for a while.

***

'Why *did* Mum stay away from Kymera for so long, Granddad? What happened?' said Olivia eventually. 'It was something to do with Uncle Nick, wasn't it?'

Granddad sighed. 'Like chalk and cheese they

were. Even as little kids. It was all a long time ago, love. Best not dwell on the past.'

'But…'

'Your Uncle Nick's not that bad, you know. He sometimes comes across as uncaring, but underneath it all…'

'He's a very nice person?'

'It's probably my fault. I know you shouldn't have favourites with your children but, well your mum, she took after me, whereas Nick took after your grandmother. Your mum loved the dogs, but Nick never bothered with them that much. Jess had a way with them like you do. It's just in you both. She could practically talk to them. I mean, Queenie and I know what each other's thinking. But with your mum it was different. Only ever seen it in the two of you. It's a rare gift you've got, Olivia. Don't waste it.

'What d'you think your mum would say about the old place now, eh? *That kitchen table looks like it's come out of a skip, Dad.* And she'd be right. It did. She'd be giving me a right rollicking. Anyway, best get on,' said Granddad, giving his eyes a sneaky wipe and heading off back to his chores.

***

Olivia looked around the kitchen, seeing it through her mum's eyes: the rickety kitchen table; the shabby old armchair that you sink down into, not because it's soft and comfortable, but because all the springs have gone in it; and the old electric cooker, with the spider trapped behind the glass front, spread-eagled and motionless. Olivia had screamed when she'd seen it that first time, until she realized it was harmless and was never going to make a run for it. Now she was almost fond of it. *Boring Brucie*, Granddad called it, because it never moved.

So different from the pretty cottage which had been Olivia's home with Mum and Dad, ivy and roses round the door, just like in the magazines.

She'd had a double bed to herself at home instead of the small single in the makeshift bedroom Granddad had constructed for her. Her wardrobe was a length of washing line stretched over one corner of the room, attached at each end to a piece of wood nailed to the wall (Granddad's brainwave). Every so often, when one coat hanger too many joined the crowd, the whole caboodle would come tumbling down and any dogs caught napping underneath ended up buried in T-shirts and jeans and occasionally even the odd frock.

Her drawers were a couple of cardboard boxes, which were always needing replacing as one dopey dog or another clambered in for a snooze, making the sides collapse. Olivia had the old washing machine on the go most days. It wasn't used to all this action and often complained with a high-pitched squeal, which brought Granddad running and shouting at the top of his voice, Who's going to pay for all this *elecktrickity*? Olivia usually ignored him or replied, *You* are, Granddad, of course, as she sent him off to the shops for some more washing powder, which he often came back without. She'd give him a good telling-off but he'd just shrug. You can't beat a good doggy smell, Olivia, he'd say.

Granddad's bedroom was even smaller than Olivia's. He'd had to divide his original one into two to accommodate her. With the double bed taking up most of the space, there was no room for even a washing-line-wardrobe, never mind a couple of cardboard boxes. *His* clothes lived in two piles in the corner of the room - one of dirty clothes and one of slightly less dirty clothes. Olivia often wandered in and picked up a heap of them with a sigh and shoved them in the washing machine, though not together with her own of course. Knowing how hard he worked, she'd sometimes iron the odd shirt for him. Granddad wasn't too fussed about his appearance, pooh-poohing any connection with his inability to find himself a girlfriend. Olivia, however, suspected he may be thinking more like a dog than a potential suitor on this occasion.

She'd once tried to give him a few pointers, but it hadn't been a huge success:

Come and sit down, Granddad. We need to have a little chat.

Aye up, sounds serious. I'm not a fan of 'little chats'. What's on your mind?

Do you not think, Granddad…?

Think what? Thinking's way overrated in my experience.

What about if we go shopping to buy you a new wardrobe?

I've no room for a wardrobe. I've nowt to put in it anyway.

Precisely my point, Granddad. We need to get you some new clothes. The wardrobe can come later.

What do *I* want with new clothes?

Well, yours *have* seen better days, you can't deny that. I don't think even a jumble sale would want your cast-offs.

There's no need for that kind of talk. I've no intention of wasting my hard-earned money on fripperies. What's the point of cleaning out the dogs in brand-new togs?

Well, you could keep the better old clothes for

that kind of stuff. But say you wanted to impress someone. A woman, maybe. Wouldn't you like a girlfriend, Granddad?

I don't need clothes to impress anybody. If people don't like me the way I am, then it's tough, he'd said, flouncing off in a huff.

However, after their 'chat', they stopped constantly running out of washing powder and a new set of undies joined the *slightly less dirty* clothes pile.

A *small* step forward as far as Olivia was concerned.

***

I don't mind anymore, Mum, that most of the furniture at Kymera is second-hand, or that the bathroom doesn't smell all nice and lemony like it did at home, or that the kitchen doesn't sparkle.

I was a bit of a nightmare when I first arrived, but I've got used to the way things are and I love being with Granddad and the dogs, especially now I've persuaded him we absolutely need the internet. We had some real rows about that. He didn't even really know what it was, but I'm gradually bringing him into the twenty-first century. He's pleased that I can look things up for him, although he pretends not to be. You know Granddad. Not that the Wi-

Fi always works. Reception's pretty patchy. Still, it's better than not having it at all.

I think you'd be happy that we've grown used to each other's ways. It's been really hard for him too. I still miss you and Dad like crazy, of course I do, but Granddad and the dogs have helped me a lot. I wish I knew the real story about you and Uncle Nick, other than he's just plain horrible. I reckon he must have done something really bad to upset you. It was awful that time we came and he turned up unexpectedly and shouted at you, I've more right to be here than you. I own half this gaff. *You sobbed all the way home in the car, saying to Dad,* We'll never be rid of him now, Max. We'll never live on Kymera now.

It was years before we went back again, but I'm so glad we did, otherwise poor Granddad would be feeling so terrible that you weren't in touch when you…I can't say the word, Mum…when you weren't here anymore.

I just hope you and Dad are happy wherever you are…

24. Lupina Tries Out Her Powers

'She's so gorgeous and sweet, isn't she, Granddad?' said Olivia as she cuddled and kissed the pup until Queenie was worried that she might suffocate it. 'She's got such a lovely soft coat and I've always wanted a black and white fluffy dog. Good old Queenie, saving her life.'

'Yes, thanks, Queenie, I owe you,' said the little pup, popping up one of her ears.

'Don't mention it, pup. It's what I'm here for,' said Queenie. 'I don't know where this "Old Queenie" nonsense has come from though. I'm not old.'

'Well, you're hardly a youngster, Queen,' said Duke.

'Quiet, numbskull,' said Queenie, still smarting from Olivia's throw-away remark.

'Whoa. Hang on. What's going on here? Are we actually talking to the runt?' said Duke, marginally on the ball for once.

'You can hear us, pup?' said Queenie, forgetting Olivia's near insult for a moment.

'Yes. It used to be only Olivia and Archie I could hear. But now I can hear you two too.'

'You were right all along, Queen. Fancy that.'

'Aren't I always, Duke? The fact that you practically died, pup, must have opened the channels of communication,' said Queenie, nodding knowledgeably.

'I'm not sure what that means,' said the pup, cocking her head on one side, 'but that nasty Pookah could have killed me if it hadn't been for you, Queenie. How *did* you bring me back to life?'

'Just one of my little spells, pup,' said Queenie, giving herself a shake. 'It goes:

"*I call upon the spirit of eternal bliss,*

To grant me the gift of a healing kiss."'

'Nice one, Queen,' said Duke. 'So that's what you were muttering. I'm almost impressed.'

***

The following morning, Archie marched into the bedroom and took hold of the pup by the scruff of her neck. Olivia had snuck her into bed with her the previous night. She thought Archie hadn't noticed but Queenie knew her man better than that. Sometimes it pays to turn a blind eye, Queenie, he said. Such strange expressions these humans had. Other times he'd be bragging about his twenty-twenty vision. Whatever…

'Come on, you, out for a wee. You'd better not have done one already,' he said, striding outside, pup dangling from his outstretched hand. The pup did not look pleased, which was understandable. After all, a dog of her calibre knows that a bed is for sleeping in and not for weeing on. But Archie couldn't be expected to know that the pup was no Queenie Two, Queenie's rather simple daughter, who caused an awful lot of mopping up in just about every room in the house when *she* was little.

Archie dumped the pup on the porch, where she contemplated the steep steps down to the garden with a look of mild concern-cum-panic. Queenie picked her up by the scruff and negotiated the climb down.

'Ta, Queenie. What now...?' said the pup as Queenie dropped her on the grass next to the duck pond.

'You heard Archie. Wees, of course. And poos. We're allowed poos in the garden first thing and before bed. Otherwise it's a discreet corner of the back field. Come on, I'll show you the best places. You follow *me*, kid. You'll soon catch on. Nowt to it.'

Queenie had her own personal favourite spot at the back of the duck pond. She liked to take her time and get it just right.

The pup hadn't learned to be picky yet and

promptly squatted and weed where she'd landed.

Duke had a rather nasty habit of weeing on top of everybody else's.

Queenie Two liked to copy Duke, not being much of a thinker herself.

That girl really should get a life.

Poor old Archie would be round later with a brush and shovel to pick up the poos. He was very meticulous like that (where other folk were concerned). Didn't miss a day. Never let it be said that anyone left their establishment with poo on their shoe.

***

Archie soon appeared on the porch. He'd had 'a good scrub' and flattened his few strands of hair down. He looked sweet. Not even a keen fan like Queenie could call him handsome. Or dark. And definitely not tall. But 'sweet', for sure.

'Get yourselves back in, you dogs,' he bellowed, not sounding as sweet as he looked.

Duke and the pup took no notice, so he bellowed some more.

'Come on, you lot,' said Queenie. 'Don't keep the boss waiting. He'll be wanting to get on with his chores.'

The pup tried to scrabble up the steps, but

they were too steep. Before Queenie could give her a helping paw, she'd shut her eyes and vanished, reappearing a nanosecond later at Archie's feet.

A look of surprise passed over Archie's face as he glanced down to see the fluffy black and white bundle of fur perched by his left foot, gazing up at him. He scratched his head and pulled a puzzled face. 'You're a smart little dog, you are, getting up those steps by yourself.'

The pup preened and puffed out her chest, but not for long as Queenie grabbed her by the scruff and strutted resolutely into the kitchen.

'Aye up, pup,' whispered Duke, who was close on her heels. 'I reckon you're in for a good roasting.'

25. ANY TAKERS FOR LA LUPINA?

KAT

Queenie takes me into the front room and Duke follows us in. Archie and Olivia are in the kitchen having a cup of tea. I know Queenie doesn't like to miss out on these things, so I'm terrified that Duke is right and I'm going to get roasted. She drops me on to the carpet.

'Please, Queenie. I don't want roasting. Please don't roast me. I'm not a chicken. I wouldn't taste good. Really I wouldn't.' I start shaking as I look at Queenie with my best pleading face, both ears flopped down.

'What are you talking about, pup? Nobody's roasting anybody. Why would I do that?'

'But Duke said…'

'Take no notice of Duke. He fancies himself as a comedian. Anyway, he just meant that you were due a telling-off. But you weren't to know, I suppose. The thing is, it's absolutely essential that there's NO magic in front of humans, even

Archie and Olivia. It's strictly forbidden. If you need to get somewhere, you walk there on your own four paws, not magically transport yourself from one place to another. Understood?'

It's still early in the day and the sun's streaming in through the windows and dancing on the furniture. I'm distracted by the flashing and twinkling of the rays of light. The smells in the room are fascinating and I wander around, sniffing in every corner.

'Pay attention when I'm speaking,' says Queenie sharply. 'This is important.'

'Sorry. What?' I focus my attention on Queenie, who has obviously not completely let me off the hook yet. After all, she is a powerful and slightly intimidating dog compared to little old me.

'I was saying that there's to be no magic, no more disappearing and reappearing - it's a dead giveaway. All behaviour in front of humans must be totally doglike. No magic whatsoever, no matter how naturally it comes to you. The role of La Lupina carries enormous responsibility. Is that clear?'

'Not really. I needed to get up the steps. "Don't keep the boss waiting," you said, although I thought that was you, Queenie. Aren't you the boss? I was just doing what you said. And what's this "Lupina" thing? I don't understand.'

Queenie gives an exasperated sigh. 'I'll explain all that properly when you're older. All you need to do for now is behave like a dog, whilst we work out where La Malina might be hiding out and what dirty tricks she might be planning.'

'"La Malina"? What's that? I wish you'd speak proper English, Queenie.' I pop up my left ear, feeling more confident now that the threat of a roasting has well and truly receded.

Queenie frowns. 'Now, you listen to me, you impudent upstart. This is serious. You may be getting on for five weeks old, but you're obviously not ready for this level of responsibility yet. Remember this though. If the Dog Council happen to hear about magic being practised willy-nilly like you've done today, then they may decide to remove your powers altogether. They do have the right to do that. Isn't that so, Duke?'

'Don't talk to me about the blooming Dog Council,' says Duke. 'Bunch of old fuddy-duddies.'

'The Dog Council?' I repeat. 'Fuddy-duddies?'

'Whatever Duke's opinion of them might be, they're ultimately in charge of the magic side of things. I might be Top Dog here on Earth, but they can override me if they decide it's in the best interests of Dogsworld.'

'They haven't a clue,' says Duke. 'Barely a brain cell between the lot of them. They wouldn't know a bone from a biscuit. Bunch of losers. Apart from Grace maybe. She's a bit of all right.'

'As if,' snorts Queenie. 'She's the daftest of the lot. You fancy her, that's all, soft lad. And I'll tell you something for nowt. She wouldn't look twice at you.'

'The green-eyed monster raising its head, Queen?'

'Get over yourself, numbskull.'

Queenie's looking really mad and I just want to get back to my mum and Olivia. I fluff out my coat and look her straight in the eyes. 'I don't want to be this Lupina, Queenie. Let some other dog do it. I'm just a little pup and I want to play and have fun. Nobody asked me if I wanted the job. Well, I don't. So there.'

'I'm afraid you have no choice, young lady,' says Queenie in a voice that makes me shiver. 'The highest honour has been granted to you and, as a member of my family, it is your duty to carry this burden with good grace and perform whatever task presents itself to the best of your ability. The future of Dogsworld rests upon your shoulders. Let me hear no more of this cowardly talk. I will not allow you to bring disgrace upon the family name.'

'Aye up, Queenie,' says Duke, 'I know you can be a bit up yourself, but that's a bit heavy even for you. To start with, you ain't even got a family name. You're just Queenie. And, as for the pup, she needs time to get used to the idea, that's all. Let's all calm down. You don't want to be blowing a gasket, Queen. After all, where would we be without our revered leader?'

'Very well,' says Queenie. 'We'll discuss all this at a later date, when the pup's grown up a bit.'

Phew. I look at Duke, who winks at me. I like him when he's nice. I actually like him even when he's not so nice because, even when he's not so nice, it feels like he actually *is* nice. *I* know what I'm talking about even if it doesn't make sense.

Queenie gives me a chilly look and goes to find Archie in the kitchen.

26. Cousin Felix Comes to Visit

Olivia was so glad it was the school holidays. She was dreading starting a new school, but luckily it would be at least a couple of months before she had to think about that. In the meantime she was determined to enjoy the summer and, hopefully, have a new friend to enjoy it with. She needed to pick her moment though.

'The pup's doing really well, isn't she, Granddad?' she said as they strolled over to the Puppy Palace, his arm draped over her shoulder and hers tucked around his waist.

'It's turning into a proper porker. We'll have to be putting it on a diet soon.'

'Oh, look at the sun, Granddad, trying to say hello from behind the clouds. It's going to be a lovely day. I feel happy today.'

'I'm glad to hear it, love, and so you should.'

A line of dogs ambled lazily behind them, sniffing here and there, not a care in the world, except for Queenie, who had a worried expression on her face.

'What's up with Queenie, Granddad?'

'Oh, you know Queenie, a law unto herself.'

As they reached the Puppy Palace, a meaty aroma wafted over from the mucky old boiler in the corner. Archie liked to give it a good clean-out once every two years or thereabouts, which wasn't really often enough.

Poor overworked Granddad. Olivia really ought to help him more. And she *would.* She'd definitely feel more like helping out if she had a little friend to keep her company.

***

'Hiya, gang,' said a voice behind them.

'Felix,' shouted Olivia, seeing him loitering in the doorway. 'What are you doing home?' This day was getting better and better. She rushed over to throw her arms around him.

'Just come to see how my Katja's doing. Dad told me about the pups,' said Felix, hugging Olivia tightly to him. 'And I don't mind seeing you two either. How's it going?'

'Ee, it's good to see you, young man,' said Granddad, wandering over and pumping Felix's hand up and down and smacking his arm. 'Fancy a nice bit of tripe for your tea?'

'Think I'll give it a miss this time, thanks, Gramps. Phwoar, that smell. Good of you to offer though.'

'Can't say you look as if you need feeding up,' said Granddad, rather rudely in Olivia's opinion. 'You're supposed to be cooking for other people at that posh catering college of yours, not scoffing it all yourself, you know. You're beginning to take after your dad.'

'What? This?' said Felix, patting his belly and laughing. 'Our Laurence has started calling me "Felix the Foodie".'

'Can't tempt you then?' said Archie, wandering over to the corner and fishing out a few pieces of tripe and breasts of lamb, which he dropped into a bucket. That drew the crowd, Queenie Two at its head. 'Here,' said Archie, picking out a few chunks and waving them about to cool them off before tossing them into the greedy mob. 'Little savages, mind you don't burn your mouths.'

'Haven't you done well, you?' said Felix, opening the door to Katja's kennel and catching her as she shot out and leapt into his arms. 'That's my girl.'

'She's *my* girl,' said Olivia.

'Huh! You love *me* best, don't you, Katja?' said Felix, laughing, as he buried his face in her fur.

'No, you don't, you love *me* best, don't you, Katja?' Poor Katja turned to look at Olivia, a troubled look on her face, then back to Felix, little ears pressed close to her head. 'Ah, we shouldn't tease her,' said Olivia, tickling her under the chin.

'We'll soon see who's favourite,' said Archie, picking out a piece of meat from the bucket and waving it in Katja's direction. Katja struggled to escape from Felix and made a beeline for Granddad.

'Well, what d'you know? It's me she loves best after all,' he said. 'Fancy that …'

'Ha, ha, Gramps. Anyway, what's this I hear about Queenie doing magic tricks? Bringing pups back to life. Spooky! I always said you were a one-off, Queenie old girl,' said Felix, bending down and giving her a pat.

'Honestly, it was a miracle, Felix.'

'That's our Queenie for you, miracle-worker.'

'I thought you didn't believe in miracles, Granddad,' said Olivia.

'It was a fluke I meant to say,' said Archie, winking at Felix.

'I know Pookah's yours and Laurence's dog, Felix, but I'm sorry, I don't like her. She's got it in for the little pup,' said Olivia. 'Can't you take her back home with you?'

'Would love to, Katja too, but they don't allow dogs where I am.'

Felix wandered over to look at the pups. 'They're a cracking lot these, aren't they? I love them at this age. They'll be ready for going before you know it, another three or four weeks.' He turned to look at Olivia. 'You know, you just need to give Pookah a chance, Liv. She's actually a nice dog once you get to know her. All dogs squabble.'

Really? A 'nice' dog? Felix may as well have said that Jack the Ripper was actually a decent sort of chap. Other than being a serial killer, who mutilated women.

'So… come on. Which is the chosen one? I bet it's that little runt sat in the corner, looking sorry for itself.'

'Chosen one?' repeated Archie.

'Well, it must have been saved for something,' said Felix. 'Isn't it you that's always saying "Everything happens for a reason"?'

'Certainly not,' snorted Archie, shaking his head.

'Hello, you,' said Felix, reaching down to pick up the pup, who was sitting by herself and not joining in with the others. 'Well, you don't *look* any different from the rest of them,' he said to her, 'apart from being weedy and having bat ears.'

'You're not weedy, are you?' said Olivia, snatching the pup off Felix. 'Take no notice of the nasty boy. You haven't got bat ears. I *love* her ears. Sometimes they stick up and sometimes one flops over, like now. And sometimes they both flop down. But you're still a gorgeous girl, aren't you?' Olivia said, rubbing noses with her. The pup lunged at Olivia's with her sharp little teeth.

'Oy! That hurt.'

'Well, what d'you expect?' said Archie. 'With a conk like that shoved in your mush, I'd be tempted to bite it myself.'

Felix and Granddad started to laugh. Clutching her throbbing nose with her free hand, Olivia couldn't help joining in. Even the pups seemed to be laughing, scampering about and giving shrill little barks.

***

'Don't you think she's adorable, Felix?' said Olivia, squeezing the pup and hugging her close.

'She *is* very sweet, I must admit,' said Felix, giving her a stroke.

'Just feel that lovely fluffy coat. Isn't she the cutest thing you've ever seen?'

'All babies are cute. It's when they grow up that the trouble starts,' said Archie. 'Mind you don't suffocate the poor thing.'

'I'll always keep her safe,' said Olivia.

'Looks like this one might be staying, eh, Gramps?'

Yes. You tell him, Felix.

'Best not let your pa hear you talking like that,'

said Archie, picking up a large slab of raw meat and tossing it in with the pups, who all rushed to seize hold of a corner, tugging and pulling and grumbling and growling, like proper little dogs.

'Down you go,' said Olivia, putting the pup back in with her sisters. 'Look, Granddad, the pup's joining in, having a really nice time. I just love her. I really do wish she could stay.'

27. WHAT'S IN A NAME?

KAT

Easy for *you* to say. You've probably got a normal name, like Emma, or Sarah, or Tom or something. Not…KAT! I can hardly bring myself to say the word. I mean, I'm a dog, aren't I? It makes me a laughing stock. What was Olivia thinking? Kat? Really? What's wrong with Princess?

All this hoo-ha about if I'd be staying or not, it was laughable, it really was. There was never any 'if' about it. Of course I was going to be staying. Duh!

Now I know Archie's not very good with money. I've heard him muttering to himself about 'elecktrickity' bills or the 'price of petrol' or 'bloomin vets' and 'daylight robbery' when he thinks no-one's listening. Next minute, it's: 'Here you are, love, have a nice chucky egg for your tea,' or, 'Help yourself to some tomatoes. You'll never taste better.' He should be selling them to people, not giving them away. That's what Queenie says anyway.

Deep down, he knows that Olivia and I are destined to be together. That's all there is to it, money or no money.

In the end he barely put up a fight. We were outside in the garden, sitting at the table. Archie had made a pot of tea and some jam and cheese butties. I'm perched on Olivia's knee. Queenie, Duke, Mum and a few other dogs are lolling about in the sun and nasty Pookah is skulking in the far corner, watching me, always watching me. As Archie pours out the tea, Oliva says casually, 'Granddad?'

'Hmm?'

'This little pup has grown really attached to me.'

'Is that right?' says Archie

'Yes, I think she'd be really upset if she had to leave. She'd pine for me. She might even die of a broken heart.'

Nice one, Olivia.

Archie gives a big sigh as he hands her a cup. That's when I know we've cracked it. 'All right,' he says. 'I suppose it can stay. BUT…it'll be *your* dog. You'll have to see to it yourself, make sure it's fed and watered…and walked.'

'Oh, I will. I'll get a paper round if you like to pay for her keep, then you won't be out of pocket.' Olivia jumps up and hugs Archie, nearly squashing me against his chest. 'Thank you, thank you, Granddad. You won't regret it. I promise. Anyway, it's a no-brainer. We belong together, me and this little pup.' Olivia dances around the garden, swaying me from side to side. I wish she'd stop because I'm starting to feel quite sick.

The other dogs seem pleased I'm staying, if all the barking is anything to go by. That horrid old Pookah doesn't join in though. She simply carries on staring at me with her piggy pink eyes. If looks could kill, I'd be a goner on the spot.

'Right then,' says Archie. 'We'd best decide on a name for the pup. Come and sit down. Now, what are we going to call her?'

That's when things start to go wrong.

'What about Trixie? We haven't had a Trixie in a while,' he says.

Trixie? Come on. I mean, do I look like a Trixie?

'Oh no, Granddad, that's boring,' goes Olivia, as she finally sits down. 'How about Hermione? Or Luna maybe?'

Not much better, I have to say, Olivia.

'What kind of names are *they* for a dog?' says Archie. 'You want a good old-fashioned dog's name like Sally.'

'Absolutely not. I rather like Fleur myself. That's French for "flower", you know.'

Princess. What about Princess? I stare at Olivia,

willing her to read my mind, but she's looking at Archie, not me.

'We don't want any poncy French names,' says Archie, rolling his eyes and taking a sip of his tea. 'You know what? I reckon we should call her Katja after her mum.'

'Wow, that's original. What? Katja Two? Like Queenie Two? D'you want her to grow up with a complex? Poor Queenie Two's so freaked out about not having her own name, she's having to eat her way through life. It's called comfort eating.' Olivia sticks out her bottom lip. She doesn't half look funny.

'What? A dog psychologist, are we now?'

'No, but it's obvious, isn't it? Even a dog needs its own name.'

'Katja's a lovely name.'

'Oh, Granddad! What about Kat? Then she's sort of named after Katja.'

NO! Princess. Princess.

'That's stupid. You can't call a dog "Cat". It's not even a proper name.'

Quite right, Archie. It definitely isn't.

'It *is* so. There's a Kat on *Eastenders*. Spelt K-A-T, not C-A-T, by the way.'

'*Eastenders*? You can't name a dog after somebody on *Eastenders*.'

'Why not? Anyway I'm not naming it after

her. I happen to like the name. I think it suits her.'

No, it doesn't. I scratch at Olivia's leg to try and get her attention.

'Stop doing that, Kat,' she says, not even glancing at me. 'And it's *my* dog, Granddad. D'you like your new name, Kat?' She lifts me up so that I'm right in front of her face. My left ear shoots up in horror. *No, no, I really, really don't.*

'See, Granddad, one of her ears has gone up. She loves it.'

I don't. Honestly, I don't. Princess. Princess. Why isn't Olivia listening to me?

'Oh well, that's a sign if ever there was one,' says Archie, laughing. 'All right. Kat it is. Let's have a toast then.'

Archie empties the contents of his cup on to the grass and reaches for a bottle of whisky he's got hidden under the table. He pours rather a lot into his cup and tops it up with lemonade. 'This'll be stewed by now,' he says, tipping the tea out from Olivia's cup into a mucky bowl that happens to be on the table and putting it down for Queenie. 'Have a cup of lemonade instead and you might as well try just a drop of whisky in it seeing as it's a special occasion.'

'To Kat,' says Archie, lifting his cup and chinking it against Olivia's.

'To Kat.' Olivia takes a sip. 'Yuck, Granddad, that's horrible. Are you sure you only put a drop in? How can you drink that? I'll never drink whisky, not if I live to be a hundred.'

'Pour it in mine then. Don't waste it. Come on, let's get a pizza in the oven. And then we can open a tin of Kitekat for the pup.'

'Ha, ha, very funny, Granddad. NOT.'

Not funny at all.

***

'I'm fed up, Queenie.' The sun has gone down and we're in the front room. Olivia's in the kitchen, trying to persuade Archie to light the fire. 'I really don't want to be a Kat.'

'What? You'd rather be called Katja Two?'

'No! I was thinking of something like Princess.'

'PRINCESS?'

'PRINCESS?' repeats Duke, rolling his eyes. 'Oh, please…'

'Hmm… What d'you say, Duke? Katja? Katja Two? Kat? Or Princess?

'Look at his face,' says Queenie, her mouth turning up as if she's about to laugh. 'I'd say this is not a subject close to the old Dog Guardian's heart.'

Duke sighs and rolls around on the rug in front of the ashes of the fire, wiggling from side to side as if trying to scratch an itch. He stands up and gives himself a shake. 'Olivia's suggestion of Fleur was the best,' he says. 'You can't beat a bit of French. If not Fleur, then my vote goes to Kat, I suppose. I'm partial to a spot of cat food. Ha! And Kat rhymes with "rat", so you've got a back-up name. Always look on the bright side, Princess Kat Rat.'

'There. Not all bad,' says Queenie.

Both she and Duke snigger.

Am I the only one not amused?

'Really…? Kat…?' I hear Duke mutter under his breath. 'Fancy being landed with a name like that.'

My Seventh Birthday

'Tea up,' shouted Granddad, emerging from the house carrying a tray with wonky-looking handles, on which was perched a bottle of milk, a packet of sugar, four rather grimy cups and a little chocolate cake with seven candles.

'Is that cake for me, Granddad? Did Mum tell you chocolate was my favourite?'

He winked at me as he set it down on the table and poured out the tea, putting two spoons of sugar in mine, just the way I like it.

'Is that tree very old, Granddad?' I pointed at the cherry tree standing tall and fierce in the corner of the garden. 'It looks very old.'

'Nearly as old as me, love. It's been here since the beginning of time. It's the garden's protector. Isn't that right, Jess?' he said, turning to look at you.

'Just like the willow tree on the back field is Kymera's protector,' you laughed. 'That's what you always used to say, Dad. And what about the treehouse? Is that still there?'

'Oh yes,' I butted in. 'Queenie…' But I was cut short by the candles setting themselves alight as if by magic, and everybody singing, Happy Birthday, dear Olivia, clapping their hands and beaming at

me. It was the best moment of my entire life.

'Make a wish,' said Granddad, as I shut my eyes and blew out the candles. 'It's your seventh birthday, so make it a special one. But be careful what you wish for. Remember, the gods have two ways of punishing us, one by not granting our wishes and the other by granting them.'

If only I'd paid more attention, maybe you and Dad would still…

28. A Contaminated Dog

'Dad? Where are you? Are you in?' boomed a voice.

'Here we go,' said Queenie to Duke, who was sitting next to her under the kitchen table, keeping cool.

Archie carried on buttering a slice of bread, as Nick's bulky figure appeared in the kitchen doorway, blocking out the sun. 'There you are. Why didn't you answer? I thought you'd be cleaning the dogs out.'

'Baggin time,' said Archie shortly.

'He's cross about that ridiculous remark Old Nick made about selling up and Archie retiring,' Queenie informed Duke, who yawned in response.

'How are them pups doing?' said Nick in a falsely jovial voice. 'Thriving, are they?'

'They're doing fine. Why d'you ask?' Slowly and deliberately, Archie spread some strawberry jam on the bread.

'Because I'm interested of course. Why else?' blustered Nick.

'Righto. Fancy a cuppa? You go sit yourself

down in the garden. I'll bring it out to you. We'll have a bit of a chinwag. Take these biscuits with you. D'you want a jam and cheese butty?'

'Na, these biscuits'll do me. Chocolate, are they? My favourite. You share your sarnie with Old Soldier there.' Nick took the packet of biscuits off the side and moved to the door. 'You come keep me company, Pookah,' he said to the bitch, who was creeping around his ankles like a witch's cat.

***

Nick sprawled untidily on the wobbly chair at the table in the garden, Pookah at his feet, as Queenie and Duke kept a watchful eye on him from the Manor steps.

Olivia emerged from the Puppy Palace, the pup, a bundle of black and white fluff, stuffed inside her jumper.

'How you doing, darling?' shouted Nick. 'Is that the runt you've got down your top? What are you like? Let's have a gander then.'

The doves bobbing about on the grass, hopeful of a crumb or two, scattered as he lurched to his feet, gut hanging over his trousers, and leaned forward to ruffle Olivia's hair.

'She's tired today,' she said, flinching and

clutching Kat tightly to her.

'Tired? Been up all night, has it? Hand it over,' said Nick, holding out his hand expectantly.

Queenie watched Olivia narrow her eyes as if willing a big hole to open and swallow Nick up. No such luck as he snatched the pup off her and proceeded to examine her eyes and ears and then roughly poked and prodded her belly, making her squeak.

Duke edged forward, growling softly, eyeing Nick up like he was a piece of prime rump steak.

Archie frowned as he came down the Manor steps carrying a tray with a pot of tea and several cups.

Even Valentino's tail had come to a standstill.

'A bit puny, but it'll do,' said Nick, oblivious to the increasingly hostile atmosphere around him. 'A lot of people prefer them smaller. Might even fetch more than the bigger ones, especially with that fluffy coat. What d'you say, Dad?'

'Now, hold on, Nick,' said Archie, glancing towards Olivia.

'Hold on, my backside,' said Nick.

'He might just get his wish,' Duke muttered to Queenie.

'Don't tell me you're going soft, Dad. This pup gets sold with the rest of them. I'm not being done out of my fair share, I'm telling you now.

This is business. I've got someone lined up for it anyway.'

'Olivia's got attached, looking after it and feeding it up. I thought we might keep it.' Archie began pouring the tea into the cups, his face expressionless.

'Keep it?' yelled Nick, his face turning purple. 'What? With all these other mutts, like that useless sheepdog, hanging around, not earning their keep? We're not having another one cluttering up the place, eating all the profits. It's our Pookah the lass needs to look out for, never mind this puny article. It's going at any rate. Here,' he said, shoving Kat back at Olivia, 'make as much fuss as you want of it for now, because soon…'

Duke moved to Olivia's side and Valentino positioned himself next to her on the other, whilst Archie went to stand behind her, laying a protective hand on her shoulder. Queenie stood shoulder to calf with Archie.

The little pup stretched up to her full height, eyes trained on Nick.

Go on, Kat! I know you shouldn't. But go on.

The air suddenly went still. Even the leaves on the trees looked stunned.

A low, grumbling growl issued forth from the dogs except for Pookah, who cowered under the table.

Nick's face grew all ugly and distorted as he took a step back. 'What's all this then?' he stammered. 'What's wrong with these dogs?'

He took another step back.

'Watch out, Nick,' yelled Archie.

'Whoa,' shouted Nick, as he lost his footing, staggered, arms flailing, and fell backwards, splat, into the duck pond.

There was a flurry of angry flapping wings from Turner and Hooch, the two Muscovy ducks, who didn't take kindly to intruders in their home.

Archie rushed forward to help Nick out.

Pookah was straight by his side.

'I'm all right, I'm all right,' he spluttered, dripping water everywhere as Archie hauled him to his feet. 'There's something wrong with that dog, I'm telling you.' Nick pointed an accusing finger in the dogs' general direction.

'What dog?' said Archie.

'That little runt dog, the one you're so keen to keep. It's evil, that's what it is. It *made* me fall in that pond.'

'Honestly, Nick, it's only a pup,' said Archie. 'You stepped back and lost your footing. You can't blame the little thing.'

'I'm telling you,' he roared. 'Its eyes went bright green and then this beam of white light shot out of them and pushed me into the pond.

You must have seen it. Tremendous force. You mark my words, that dog is contaminated.'

'White light…? Contaminated…?' repeated Archie, shaking his head. 'Are you feeling all right, Nick? You didn't bump your head when you fell, did you? Come and sit down over here a minute.'

'No, I didn't. And I didn't fall neither. I was pushed. By, by…THAT,' he snarled, pointing at the pup again.

'I think you're right, Granddad,' said Olivia. 'Uncle Nick *must* have bumped his head. He should go home and rest.'

29. Nick Has Another Shock

Instead of packing him off home, as Queenie would have done, Archie brought Nick a whisky to calm his nerves and warm him up. Looking like he'd been sucking on a particularly sour lemon, he sat back at the old iron table, green slime and miscellaneous pond life dripping from him.

'What's been going on here then?' said a voice. 'What happened to *you*, Dad?'

As Felix came around the corner, Olivia ran to meet him. 'Your dad fell in the pond, Felix. He's blaming this little pup.'

'What…? How did he manage that? You all right, Dad? Shouldn't you be getting out of those wet clothes? You don't want to catch your death.'

'I'm not so sure about that,' muttered Duke to Queenie.

'There's something wrong with that pup. It's contaminated.'

'Contaminated…? Get away. It's a little cutey.' Felix tickled the pup under her chin. 'Just feel that lovely soft coat. It's really taken to you, hasn't it, Liv? Have you decided to keep it?'

The pup shrank back against her, as Olivia

glanced towards Old Nick, who shook his head and said, 'I didn't have you down as selfish, my girl. After all your granddad's done for you - taking you in and giving you a home. He didn't *have* to do that, you know. Lots wouldn't. He could do with the money. We all could.'

'Well, I'm keeping it, so there,' yelled Olivia. 'And there's nothing you can do about it. Granddad built this place and he gets to decide, not you.'

'Well, you cheeky little madam. You watch that tongue of yours, or else…'

'Or else what? I'm not frightened of you.'

Queenie had never seen Olivia look so mad. She saw the pup suddenly go stiff in Olivia's arms. *Oh-oh, Forbidden Incident Alert.* Before she could act, the rickety chair Nick was sitting on started to wobble like there was a mini-earthquake under it, Nick wobbling with it like a giant green jelly.

'Ow, ow, ow,' he yelled, as he crash-landed.

Pookah rushed to his side, but Nick waved her away and held out an arm for Felix to pull him to his feet.

'Not your day today, is it, Nick?' said Archie. 'One whisky too many?'

'It's nowt to do with the whisky,' yelled Nick. 'It's that dog again. It wants getting rid of. Contaminated, that's what it is.'

'Anyway,' said Nick, once he was settled with yet another whisky, 'there's something else we need to discuss, Dad.'

'Oh aye, and what's that then, lad?'

Nick glanced at Felix. 'Now I know you love the place, Dad, but it's getting too much for you now. I'm sorry to say it, but you're getting too old for this game. I really think we need to sell up. I know someone who'd give us a very good price for the land. They approached me when all this fracking business was going on.'

'They approached you or you approached them?' Archie's tone was icy. 'Anyway the fracking's all gone to pot now. Some fella came down here once, mouthing off about it and how rich we'd be if we sold to them. I soon sent him packing.'

'Aye, well the chap I know's still interested, fracking or no fracking.'

Archie banged his fist on the table. 'And you can tell him where he can stick his interest. We're not selling. *I'm* not selling and you can't sell the place without my say-so.'

'Nobody wants to sell the place from under you, Dad,' Old Nick patted Archie's arm, 'but just think what you could do with *your* half. A nice house for you and Olivia, with a bit of land maybe. You could even keep some of the dogs.'

Queenie glanced over at Olivia's horror-struck face.

'Wouldn't you like a nice house to live in, Olivia? Instead of slumming it here?' said Nick with a cheery grin as if they hadn't been squabbling moments earlier.

'No, I wouldn't,' she practically spat at him. 'This is our home, Granddad's and mine. We don't want to live anywhere else.'

'Felix agrees with me that it would be the best thing, don't you, Felix?'

Felix kept his eyes on the ground and mumbled something incoherent. Queenie was itching to give them both a bite. Except she wasn't that kind of dog.

'Oh, does he now? With all due respect, this has nothing to do with Felix. And if that's the way he feels, then maybe he should stay away.'

'Hey, Gramps, there's no need to be like that,' said Felix, looking miserable. 'I just thought you might want a less busy life, do something you've always wanted to do instead of working all the time.'

'This *is* what I've always wanted to do,' said Archie slowly and deliberately. 'This is exactly what I've always wanted to do. I'm looking after dogs. I'm saving their lives. Is that good enough for you?'

Olivia looked uncomprehendingly at Felix. 'Felix, how can you…?'

Felix jumped up. 'Sorry, Gramps. Sorry, Olivia. I have to go. I'll see you at home, Dad.'

Queenie thought she saw a tear run down his cheek as he stumbled away.

***

'You're burying your head in the sand, Dad. This place can't survive. None of us are making enough to live on. Janey's not happy.' Nick shook his head slowly from side to side.

'Well, tell Janey to get herself a job then,' said Archie coldly. 'Anyway we'll make a fair bit with the pups. That should keep our heads above water.'

'It's a drop in the ocean. You know that, Dad. It won't be long before we're back where we started. You're too soft.'

Queenie nudged Duke as she saw Olivia flush bright red. 'It might help if *you* did something for a change instead of leaving it all to Granddad,' she shouted.

'Olivia,' said Granddad, putting a restraining hand on her arm.

'Well, it's true. You're nothing but a…a… parasite.' Tears sprang to Olivia's eyes and Kat stiffened again in her arms.

Archie stood up. 'Enough's been said. I think it's time you went, Nick. But I want to make something quite clear first. We shan't be selling Kymera. And we *shall* be keeping this little pup, whether you like it or not.'

'Oh, please yourself,' said Nick, lumbering to his feet and stomping off, shoes squelching, hair plastered to his head and dollops of sludgy green gunk hanging from his clothes.

As he reached the pond, he turned back and bellowed, 'It's not over. You haven't heard the last of this, young lady. I won't be spoken to like that by some jumped-up lass.'

'There goes the monster from the green lagoon,' said Queenie to Duke. But neither of them were in the mood for jokes.

30. Olivia Goes Hot

'I know you were annoyed with your Uncle Nick. I was pretty mad with him myself, but I don't like you speaking to him like that. You need to show some respect. You're letting yourself down, Olivia.'

'He doesn't exactly show *you* respect.' Olivia felt the heat rush to her face and tears began to prickle behind her eyes. She hated it when Granddad was cross with her.

'That's for me to deal with. Not you.'

'I always feel he doesn't really like me, like I shouldn't be here.' An escapee tear trickled down her face.

'It's not you he's a problem with really,' said Granddad in a kindlier tone. 'It was your mother and you're so like her.'

'He can't *make* you sell, can he, Granddad?'

'No. I suppose he might be able to sell *his* half. That could cause us a problem. I need to look into that.'

'He wouldn't do that,' said a voice behind them.

Olivia and Archie both turned to look at Felix, who was standing near the pond, looking rather sheepish. 'Look, I'm sorry about before. Dad thinks it's the best thing to do. He's worried about you, that's all. But if you don't want to sell, I'm sure he'll understand. Anyway I'd really miss the place.' He held out his arms. 'Give us a hug, Liv?'

Olivia looked at Granddad, who nodded. She wandered over and Felix squeezed her close. Kat, who was squashed between them gave a little whimper. They both laughed. 'Friends?' said Felix, giving Olivia's hair a ruffle.

'Friends,' said Olivia.

Felix went over to Granddad and held out his hand. After a moment's pause, Granddad stretched out his and they ended up in a brief hug too.

'I'd hate to fall out with you, Gramps.' Felix's eyes filled with tears.

'Never mind all that. Let's talk about something that really matters. Are you courting yet? You must be getting on for twenty now. Time you had a girlfriend.'

'Courting? Honestly, Gramps. What does that even *mean*?'

'Walking out … you know.'

Felix rolled his eyes at Olivia and sucked in his cheeks.

She gulped and gave a little smile. *Dear Felix.*

She could never not have him in her life.

'No, no girlfriend, Gramps, nobody special anyway.'

'Your dad says Laurence has managed to con some poor girl into going out with him. What d'you think of that then, Olivia?'

'Nothing?' She could feel herself going hot again. Why did Granddad always have to insinuate things about her and Laurence? It was so childish. Honestly, she could kill him sometimes. OK, she may have had a bit of a crush on him when she was a lot younger, and she may just have googled cousins marrying each other. But she was so over it now.

'You wanted to marry him when you were little. Remember that?' insisted Granddad. 'You used to say…'

'Leave her be, Gramps, she was only a bit of a kid. And you've got to admit our Laurence is quite the charmer.'

'Oh, I know *that*, Felix. He's got the gift of the gab all right.'

'That's nice for Laurence to have a girlfriend,' said Olivia. 'What's she like? Is she pretty?' It was only polite to show an interest. She'd no intention of listening properly to the answer.

'Yes, she's pretty all right, his usual type - long blonde hair and big baby-blue eyes. She actually seems a really nice girl.'

'Oh, really?' Not exactly what she wanted to hear. She smiled brightly.

'Aye, too nice for him,' said Granddad.

'Not a patch on you though, Liv,' said Felix. 'Don't worry, he'll soon tire of her. They never last long. That's the trouble with Laurence, he gets bored easily.'

'Why should *I* worry? I don't care *who* Laurence goes out with. I was only making conversation, that's all. I'm glad for him.' Olivia shrugged as if she found the subject of who Laurence was seeing rather tedious.

'Huh,' said Granddad.

'He's been around this weekend as it happens. Come to share the good news about his exam results,' said Felix. 'Floated in and floated out again apparently. Didn't he pick our Pookah up? I could have sworn I saw her in the car with him earlier.'

Suddenly a band of little men began hammering away inside Olivia's chest. Laurence was *home*?

'Well, *we* haven't seen him,' said Granddad. 'Not unless he came and took her whilst I was busy and your father brought her back. She was in the kitchen this morning. She keeps out of the way mostly. You know her and Queenie never hit it off. In fact she doesn't really get on with any of the other dogs. Bit of a loner.'

'Funny, it looked like Pookah, though I haven't seen our Laurence to speak to,' said Felix. 'Don't think I register on his "interesting people" radar.'

'You're worth ten of him, if not eleven, and don't you forget it, lad,' said Granddad, shaking his head. 'What's he come home for anyway? I thought he was too posh for the likes of us these days.'

'Don't be hard on him, Gramps. He loves coming home. And he loves coming to Kymera. I'm sure he'll be down to see you both before he goes back.'

'Tell him not to do us any favours.'

'Granddad,' said Olivia.

'Well, I suppose someone will be pleased to see him,' said Granddad with a wink, as Olivia fanned herself with her free hand.

31. Kat Meets Oberon and a Man Comes to Visit

'Is it all right if I take Kat out on a ride with me, Granddad?'

'Isn't that a bit dangerous, love?'

'Oh? D'you think so?'

'Yes, I should leave it until she's a bit older.'

Olivia put her hand over the pup's nose to stop her licking her face. 'Maybe you're right. I'll just take her round while I'm grooming Oberon. It's about time they met each other. I'm sure they're going to be great friends.'

'And take that screeching nit with you. He's getting right on my wick.'

Olivia laughed as she put a calming hand on Duke's head. 'All right, Duke, quieten down. Yes, we'll be going out with Oberon in a bit. Come on, come with me.'

Olivia, headed off, followed by Duke who was still bouncing around, making a lot of noise. Valentino and Queenie Two strolled after them, whilst Queenie stayed in the kitchen with Archie.

Oberon was standing with his head poking out over the stable door and did several whinnies, like he was saying hello, when he caught sight of Olivia and her entourage.

'And hello to you too, Oberon,' said Olivia, unlatching the door. Oberon strode out, nodded at Duke and began nuzzling Olivia.

'Look who's come to see you today, Oberon,' said Olivia, drawing out the pup from inside her jacket. 'This is Kat, our new friend. She's going to be coming out with us today. But don't tell Granddad. He doesn't approve.'

Oberon whinnied loudly and nodded his head up and down a few times before putting his nose up to the pup and blowing on her.

Kat yipped excitedly and licked the end of Oberon's nose.

'Oh, I'm glad you two seem to like each other,' said Olivia, as Kat's right ear shot up and down several times, before finally staying erect.

'Do you want to sit on Oberon's back while I give him a quick brush?' said Olivia, placing the pup gently down and patting Oberon. 'You look after Kat, now. Make sure she doesn't fall. Don't be frightened, Kat. I'll be watching.'

Kat didn't look in the least bit frightened. In fact she seemed very comfortable indeed, as Olivia gave Oberon the once-over with the brush, removing a few tangles from his jet-black mane and smoothing out his tail. Kat gave the odd little grumble and Oberon responded with a couple of neighs. Even Duke joined in with a few growls.

'It's like you lot are talking to each other. I'd love to know what you're all saying,' said Olivia, laughing as she gave Kat and Oberon a mint each and dropped a few on the floor for Duke, Queenie Two and Valentino. 'I hope it's an interesting conversation.'

Duke barked as if acknowledging the observation and the treats.

Queenie Two had a little go at Valentino, no doubt thinking that all the mints were hers by rights. Valentino backed off, having had altercations over food with Queenie Two in the past and always come off worst. 'You
shouldn't always let her win, Val,' remonstrated Olivia. 'That Queenie Two's a little piggy wiggy.'

She was about to saddle Oberon up when Archie came rushing round, out of breath. 'Can you hang on a bit, love, before you go out on the nag? I've run out of bread and milk and I just want to nip to the shops. I don't want to leave the place unmanned, what with having the little pups. Save me locking everywhere up.'

'No, that's fine, Granddad. I'm sure Duke won't mind waiting,' said Olivia, although Duke looked like he most definitely *would* mind. 'And at least Kat's met Oberon now.'

'Aye, well that's the main thing,' said Archie, giving Olivia a wink. 'I won't be long.'

Queenie Two was sniffing around the stable in the hope of hoovering up any stray mints or nuts, watched by a bored-looking Valentino, as Olivia patted Oberon on the rump to send him off into the field for a graze. He nudged Duke and snuffled over the pup again, before turning and setting off at a canter.

Duke trailed behind Olivia, looking dejected, as she made her way back to the Manor. 'Cheer up, Duke. We'll be able to go soon,' said Olivia.

Duke wagged his tail slowly as if he'd heard her, before turning to gaze longingly after Oberon.

***

'Anybody home?' Olivia jumped as a face appeared at the kitchen door.

A smartly-dressed man in his late twenties or early thirties stepped in. 'I'm Jonathan Tate, at your service, little Miss,' he said, doing a little bow. 'Is the boss about?'

Olivia grimaced at the 'little Miss' remark. 'No, he won't be back for a while yet. Can *I* help?'

'I hear you've got some pups for sale.'

Duke growled menacingly.

'Shush, Duke,' said Olivia. She turned back

to the man. 'Yes, I can show you them if you like. But they won't be ready to leave their mum for another couple of weeks at least.'

As she led him over to the Puppy Palace, Olivia wondered whether she was doing the right thing. Kat had gone very stiff in her arms and Duke was still grumbling. Granddad would be pleased though if she managed to make a sale. Only she wasn't sure the man was right for the pups. There was something shifty about him. He was wearing the wrong sort of clothes for a start. Kymera was hardly the place for pinstripe suits. And he kept looking all around him as if he was casing the joint. At least that's what it felt like. Olivia wondered if she were being paranoid.

'You live here, do you?' he said.

'Yes,' she replied in a clipped tone. 'I live here with my granddad.'

Inside the Puppy Palace, Olivia indicated the pups clustered around Katja, who growled when the man looked in.

'Not very friendly, is she?'

'She doesn't know you,' responded Olivia. 'She's naturally protective of her pups. Would you like me to get one for you to look at?'

The man shifted uncomfortably. 'What about the one you're holding?'

'I'm afraid this one's not for sale.'

The man stretched out his hand and Kat snapped at his fingers.

'Not friendly either.'

'Dogs need to get to know you,' Olivia informed him politely.

'So, how much are you selling them for?'

'A thousand pounds each.' Olivia made up a figure that she thought would put the man off. 'And we do of course have to inspect any potential homes for the pups to make sure they're suitable. We can't be letting them go to just anyone.'

'Is that right? Nice to know you're fussy. It's quite a place you have here. Fancy showing me round, young lady?' The man winked and gave her a lecherous smile. 'It seems only fair if you're going to be looking at my quarters.'

Duke started barking and the man backed away towards the door.

'I think it's best if you come back when my granddad is here,' said Olivia, her heart thudding in her chest. *What did this man want?*

'Fair enough.' The man held up both hands. 'I'll come back at a more convenient time. Nice to meet you, Olivia.'

With that he strode off down the path, leaving Olivia wondering how he knew her name.

My Seventh Birthday

'Please may I leave the table, Granddad?' I asked through a mouthful of cake. 'I'd like to go exploring some more.'

'Well, now, how could I refuse a polite request like that? You've obviously been well brought up, a credit to your mum and dad.'

'Apart from speaking with her mouth full. Honestly, Olivia. Remember your manners.'

But both you and Dad were smiling.

'You go with Olivia,' said Granddad to Queenie, who was sitting at his feet. 'Show her round the place. Don't let her get into any mischief, mind. Make sure you look after her.'

'Look after me? I don't need looking after,' I said, leaping up. 'Come on, then, Queenie.'

She led me all over, down winding paths that randomly snaked off to an unexpected oasis of wildflowers and roses, or a group of chickens bobbing around, pecking amongst the grass, unbothered by the dogs milling about, who knew to leave them be. When the stable came into view, I noticed a glossy, black head poking over the door. Remember me telling you about meeting Oberon for the first time, Mum? He neighed as soon as he saw me, as if he recognised me from somewhere. You laughed when I told you it sounded like he was saying 'Olivia'. I rushed over and he bent his head down to nuzzle my hair and nibble my ear.

Queenie nosed me away as if she had other things she wanted to show me. Eventually we happened upon the dog cemetery. That felt so peaceful. Until I came across a headstone that said:

'Here lies Molly,
Loyal companion to Jessica,
Deeply loved and never forgotten.
RIP dearest friend. Miss you always.'

It made me cry. I asked you about Molly, Mum, when we got home, but you looked upset and said, 'Not now, Olivia. One day I'll tell you about her'.

And now that day will never come…

32. Olivia Has a Plan and Archie Gives Her a Present

'Any problems while I've been out, love?' Granddad came striding into the kitchen, followed by Queenie and plonked a bag of shopping on the side. 'Sorry, I've been a bit longer than I thought. I bumped into Nick in the shop and he kept me talking. He even wanted me to go back to his for a cuppa. He took some fobbing off I can tell you.' He turned to face Olivia. 'What's up? You look a bit peaky. Has something happened?'

'A man's been here. I didn't like him. The dogs didn't like him either.'

'A man? What man?' Granddad narrowed his eyes and frowned. 'What man, Olivia?'

Olivia wrinkled her nose as if it had suddenly been assaulted by a bad smell. 'He said he wanted a pup, but he seemed dodgy to me, all dressed up in his suit. Duke growled at him. Katja did too. Even little Kat snapped at him.'

Kat, who'd been snoozing on Olivia's lap, sat up at the mention of her name.

'He wanted me to show him round the place. Anyway I told him to come back when you were here. I also told him that the pups were a thousand pounds each because I didn't want him to have any of them. Are you mad at me, Granddad?'

Archie laughed, but not a proper laugh. He looked worried. 'What did he look like, this man?'

Olivia described him - his pinstripe suit, his slicked back hair, his cocky manner, his sleazy smile. 'He was a slimeball, Granddad. He really gave me the creeps. Oh, and he knew my name.'

'Did he now?' Granddad sat down at the table looking thoughtful. 'I wonder if it's the same fracking slimeball, who tried to persuade me to sell the place to him once. I just hope Nick hasn't sent him to try and twist my arm. If he comes back again, I'll soon show him the door. And we won't be selling him any pups either. Not if none of you took to him.'

'Good,' said Olivia. 'And you should think about checking people's homes before you let them have a pup anyway. That's what I told him you did. Interview them properly. It's a no-brainer.' She nodded firmly and Kat gave a squeaky bark like she was backing her up.

'And when have I got time for all that? When there's proper work to be done.'

'That can be *my* job,' said Olivia. 'Which brings me on to my next point.'

'Hark at you, Miss Bossy Boots,' said Archie

with a smile. 'Come on, let's hear it then.'

'Well…I've been thinking about those abandoned dogs in the Big Kennels.'

'What about them, love?' Granddad put his hands on the table and heaved himself to his feet. He seemed weary all of a sudden, like everything was getting on top of him.

'You sit down, Granddad. You've time for a cuppa. I'll make you one. I can go out with Oberon tomorrow.' Archie lowered himself back down on to the chair with a sigh as Olivia gave him Kat to hold and went to put the kettle on. She rinsed out a couple of cups in the sink and glanced back at him. 'I was thinking,' she carried on, 'those dogs will have had a pretty horrible life if they've been made to fight and they're probably scared. They deserve better than to spend the rest of their lives in a kennel with no-one to love them. It's a shame for them.'

'I let them out in the runs a couple of times a day, but I don't have the time to do anything else with them, what with everything I have to see to,' said Granddad defensively.

Olivia came back to the table and, after plonking down the teapot and a couple of cups, sat down opposite him. 'Let *me*, Granddad. I can bring them round. I know I can.'

'I don't know, love,' said Archie, pouring

out the tea. 'They don't trust people. Fighting is probably all they've ever known, right from being pups.'

'I can do it, Granddad. I was all right with that Cliff dog, wasn't I? Please, Granddad. Let me try.' Olivia put on her best pleading look for him. 'I can't bear to think of them stuck in there for the rest of their time on earth. It seems cruel.'

'I've saved those dogs' lives,' said Archie indignantly.

'I know that Granddad, but it's not really much of a life for them, is it? Just think. If I could get them socialized…'

'Oh? Socialized, is it?'

'Yes, Granddad. Socialized. Then we might be able to find them their forever homes. Surely it's worth a try?'

Archie paused, took off his cap, gave his head a scratch and put it back on.

Olivia, sensing victory, persisted. 'It would free up some kennels for the boarders as well. Then that would bring in a bit more money.'

Archie looked down at Queenie, who was sitting at his feet. 'What d'you reckon, Queenie?'

Queenie yapped enthusiastically.

Little Kat joined in with some squeaky barks and a lot of ear movement. Up, down. Up, down.

'You see, both Queenie and Kat think it's a

good idea,' said Olivia.

'Aye, all right. We'll give it a go. I mean, if Queenie and Kat are in favour, who am I to argue?'

'This dogfighting doesn't still go on, does it, Granddad?'

'I'm afraid so, love. The world can be a wicked and cruel place.'

Olivia gasped, a horrified look on her face. 'I thought it was banned. I thought…'

'It still happens undercover. It's people that are to blame, not the poor dogs. They're just victims themselves.' Archie knocked back his tea and shook his head. 'I won't have time to watch you while you go through all this "socializing" business,' he said, doing the imaginary inverted commas thing with his fingers. 'I'll keep an eye on you the first couple of times, but then you're on your own.'

'I'll be fine, Granddad. As you're always saying, I've a way with the dogs.'

Granddad could tell when he was beaten. 'Got an answer for everything, you, haven't you? Now make me a jam and cheese butty before I change my mind.'

Olivia clapped her hands excitedly and all the dogs in the kitchen began barking.

Granddad looked at her affectionately.

'Hang on a minute,' he said, getting up, 'I've got something for you.' He ambled off into his bedroom and emerged minutes later with a packet wrapped in brown paper. 'Here you are, love. It's not new, but it *is* special. I was going to save it for your birthday, but then I thought you might like it now.'

It almost felt like her birthday as Olivia tore off the paper and pulled out a purple amulet on a silver chain. 'Oh, Granddad, that's beautiful.' She touched the jewel with delicate fingers and it began to glitter and flash all the colours of the rainbow. 'Oh, wow,' she gasped. 'Thank you so much, Granddad.'

'It belonged to your mother. She reckoned there was something magical about it, that it protected her. From what, I don't know. She told me she found it in the treehouse. A gift from the fairies, she said.' Archie smiled. 'She loved that treehouse Practically lived up there. D'you know? She never took that necklace off. Up until she left. She didn't want to take it with her. Said it belonged here. Gave it to me for safekeeping. "Dad," she said, "I'd love to live on Kymera one day. When that day comes, I'll ask you for it back."' Archie sighed and cleared his throat. 'We'll never see that day now, so I think she would want *you* to have it, Olivia. Guard it with your life.'

Olivia's eyes swam with tears. 'I will, Granddad. I definitely will. I've got the perfect box for it when I'm not wearing it.' She clasped the amulet to her heart and was suffused with a feeling of such exquisite bliss that it completely banished the sadness that had been threatening to overwhelm her.

33. Olivia in Love

Olivia stood gazing out of the kitchen window, deep in thought, Kat in her arms. 'O-M-G!'

Queenie and Duke, who had their heads together in the corner of the kitchen like they were in the middle of an important conference, looked over in her direction.

'Laurence is here,' she whispered to them, 'with Felix. OMG.'

She set the pup down on the dilapidated old chair, heart going like a sledge-hammer, and rushed into the bedroom to grab a freshly ironed, purple 'I Love Dogs' T-shirt from off the bed and the box containing the amulet. Going into Granddad's bedroom, she held the T-shirt up against herself, sucking in her cheeks and pursing her lips at her reflection in the full-length mirror in the corner of the room. She dragged off the baggy top she was wearing (one of Aunt Janey's old cast-offs) and adjusted the tiny bra she'd secretly bought off the internet. Just need some bits and bobs for school, she'd told Granddad, who'd grudgingly handed over his credit card, the one the lady bank manager had persuaded him was a vital asset to a businessman of his standing and which generally languished alone and unloved at the back of the kitchen drawer. He hadn't asked any questions, fortunately.

Pulling the T-shirt over her head and patting it down, Olivia turned from side to side as she looked at herself in the mirror. Peering up closely, she pinched her cheeks and scrunched up her hair, going for the casually dishevelled look. Unwrapping the piece of purple silk protecting the amulet, she paused briefly before fastening the silver chain carefully at the back of her neck. As she gazed into the mirror again, her reflection shimmered slightly along with the image she was seeing reflected back at her. Instead of Granddad's bedroom with the double bed and the picture of Granddad's parents above it, she found herself looking into her old bedroom at home with the turquoise and purple wallpaper, covered in dragons, unicorns, owls and fairies. She could see her bed, Bow Wow, her toy dog, perched on the pillow, and her sparkly purple wardrobe and drawers. She took a step back, clutching the amulet, and shut her eyes. Opening them again, she was faced once more with the reflection of Granddad's bedroom. No turquoise and purple wallpaper. No sparkly purple wardrobe. No Bow Wow.

The thought of seeing Laurence must have turned her head…

Back in the kitchen, she picked up Kat, tucked her under her arm and sauntered out into the garden, Queenie and Duke following behind.

Felix and Laurence were sitting at the old iron table, Pookah at their feet, in between the two of them.

'Hey, Good Looking,' said Laurence, getting up and ruffling her curls, 'what's cooking?'

Olivia giggled self-consciously as she gazed into those dark, smouldering eyes with their luscious long lashes. His swathe of black hair curled down on to his shoulders and he was wearing a startlingly white suit and a black silk shirt. Even his black patent shoes looked like they were fresh from a visit to the shoe shiner. Hardly fitting attire for Kymera, but Olivia was spellbound. It was Heathcliff himself, transformed from savage to gent, returned to claim his one true love. That would be Olivia, naturally. She'd watched *Wuthering Heights* loads of times with Queenie and Duke. The three of them couldn't take their eyes off the screen, Olivia reduced to a blubbering mess by the end when Cathy dies in Heathcliff's arms, Queenie blinking back the tears and Duke mysteriously assailed by a coughing fit.

***

Felix stood up and hugged her close. Olivia was glad they'd sorted out the misunderstanding earlier. Dear Felix. Always in Laurence's shadow. Neither as handsome nor as brainy. But so warm and affectionate. This would never do. In love with two brothers at the same time? And both of them her cousins.

'This is the pup I was telling you about,' said Felix to Laurence, 'brought back from the dead by Queenie.'

'Wow. Miracle pup. May I take a look?' said Laurence, with a suave smile.

Olivia handed the pup over and sat herself down next to Felix, who draped his arm around her. Leaning into him, she watched Laurence as he held Kat at arm's length and scrutinised her. 'So, what are you going to call her, Liv?'

'Kat.' Olivia made them laugh as she recounted the pup-naming incident with Granddad.

'Kat…? Great name for a dog,' said Laurence.

'Certainly a step-up from Sally or Trixie,' said Felix. 'What's Gramps like?'

'What's all this?' shouted Granddad, as he came out of the Puppy Palace with Katja, who rushed over to them. 'What are you two reprobates doing here?'

'How are you, Granddad? Still devoting your life to the dogs, I see,' said Laurence, handing the pup back to Olivia and stepping forward and proffering his hand.

'And what's wrong with that?' said Granddad, shaking the outstretched hand unenthusiastically. 'I suppose you think you're a cut above because you're at university?'

'Give me a break, Granddad. I've only come to say hello to you and Liv and have a look at the pups.'

'Hmmph,' said Granddad. 'That's why you're here, is it? Not part of the grand scheme of trying to get me to sell the place, then? Well, it won't work. You can gang up all you like.'

34. A Footling Dandy

Laurence shifted about in his chair and ran a hand through his dark, silky locks. 'Nobody's ganging up on anybody, Granddad. Dad did tell me about the offer he'd had. You should at least consider it. What harm can it do?'

Olivia stiffened and Kat gazed at her with a worried look on her face.

Katja leapt up on to the bench and snuggled between Olivia and Felix. 'This is the best dog on the place,' said Felix, laughing awkwardly in an obvious attempt to disperse the tension in the air. Katja burrowed under his arm, bottom protruding and tail wagging furiously.

'I'm considering nothing,' said Granddad angrily.

There was an uncomfortable silence as both people and dogs turned to look at Archie, who sat there glowering stubbornly.

Olivia cleared her throat. 'How are you doing anyway, Laurence? How's university treating you?' She supposed this was what they called 'polite conversation'.

'It's a doddle, Liv. I'm having a fine old time. I've missed seeing *you* though,' he said hastily.

'Thought I'd pop down and take you and this little pup out for a ride in my new Jag whilst I'm back for a few days. We can have a proper catch-up.'

'Well, you can think again,' said Archie. 'And how can *you* afford a Jag when you're supposed to be a student?'

'Called in a favour from a friend, Granddad, and it's not this year's model. It's quite an old one actually. Good for my image. It's all about street cred these days. Don't you fancy a little trip out, Liv?'

'I think I should stay here, thanks, Laurence,' said Olivia in a small voice, glancing at Archie. 'I told Granddad I'd try and tame some of the abandoned dogs in the Big Kennels, so he can perhaps find them new homes and save money on feeding them.'

'Aren't some of those dogs quite vicious?' said Felix, looking anxiously towards Archie.

'Is it safe?' said Laurence. 'I wouldn't want my best girl getting bitten.'

'I'll be there supervising,' said Archie. 'Do you really think I'd put Olivia in any danger? It'll be safer than going out in the car with the likes of you.'

Katja clambered on to Olivia's knee, obviously sensing that she was on the verge of tears. She and

Kat snuggled up together.

'Blimey, Granddad. Chill out,' said Laurence, getting to his feet. 'I'm actually a pretty good driver.'

'"Chill out"? Don't you be telling *me* to chill out. You watch your manners, you young pup. Show some respect.'

Laurence shook his black mane, Oberon-fashion, and shrugged. 'I'm going to get going,' he said. 'I'll come again when you're in a better mood, Granddad. Stuff to do anyway. You coming, Felix?'

Felix nodded and gave Olivia a hug.

'So you're *both* going? You've only just come.'

'Don't worry, Liv. We'll see you soon,' said Laurence, leaning in and kissing her on the cheek. 'Oh,' he said, stepping back, 'what's that you're wearing round your neck?'

'It used to be Mum's,' murmured Olivia. 'Granddad gave it to me.'

As Laurence reached out and touched the necklace, it glowed vividly, just like it had when Olivia first held it.

'Wow, that's beautiful,' said Laurence, stepping forward and kissing her other cheek. 'Just like you,' he whispered in her ear.

Olivia giggled stupidly, feeling herself going as red as one of Granddad's tomatoes. She tried to visualise herself standing barefoot on hot coals in an attempt to drag the heat down from her face to her feet. Somebody had once told her it was a sure-fire way to make you pale and interesting again. They were lying. She felt ridiculous, like a star-struck groupie. With a very red face. She couldn't even speak. Felix winked at her, making matters worse as her face blended in even more neatly with her purple T-shirt. How embarrassing was *that*?

***

Archie was looking decidedly grumpy as they accompanied Laurence and Felix round the front. Pookah followed them over to the car, white and gleaming in the sun, hood down, showing off the mahogany leather interior.

'Quite old, you say?' said Granddad.

Laurence laughed as he put one hand on the top of the door and expertly vaulted into the driver's side. Pookah looked wistfully at the seat next to him and Olivia felt a teeny twinge of empathy for her, both of them longing for the same thing.

Felix picked Pookah up and gave her a cuddle. 'Now you look after Olivia, our Pookah,' he said.

'Aren't *you* going to say goodbye to your dog,

Laurence?' said Granddad.

Laurence shrugged as he glanced at his reflection in the driving mirror.

'Not worried about messing up your nice white suit, are you?' said Granddad, wandering off and chuntering to himself about people coming down to Kymera in their Sunday best, something a proper Dogwalla would never do.

***

'You were really mean to Laurence, Granddad,' said Olivia, catching up with him outside the Cattery. 'Anybody would think you didn't like him.'

'Maybe I don't.'

'Why? What's he ever done to you?'

'He's just a bit of a smart Alec. Loves himself too much. Needs taking down a peg or two, that's all.'

'That's not fair, Granddad. He's nice, Laurence. I like him.'

'He's a footling dandy,' said Archie, opening one of the Cattery cage doors and tickling its purring, grey-coated occupant on the head.

'He's a what?'

'I'm sorry, love, I know you've a soft spot for Laurence. Take no notice of this old goat. I'm that way out today. It's all this talk about selling up. It's really getting on my nerves.'

'Well, I'm on your side, Granddad.' Olivia took hold of his free hand and gave it a squeeze. 'I'll help you make some money. We'll sort out those fierce dogs and find them homes, sell the pups and get the place looking more presentable. Then we can stay here forever. I think Felix and Laurence mean well. It'll be Uncle Nick who's getting at them.

'Poor Laurence. A "footling dandy" …?' Olivia laughed. 'You've just made that up, haven't you? Honestly, Granddad, what are you like?'

35. The First Steps

Olivia hoped Laurence hadn't taken offence at her refusal to go for a ride in the car with him. There was nothing she'd have liked better, but she couldn't upset Granddad any more than he already was. She wouldn't think about that now. There was work to be done.

She put on her oldest clothes. Her plan was to get the fierce dogs used to her gradually, maybe just sit quietly with them for a while and try and gain their confidence so that they realized she was no threat.

She approached the Big Kennels and shouted Granddad. He soon appeared at the entrance and opened the door for her. 'I'm just going to carry on cleaning out and swapping the dogs over in the runs. You do what you have to do, but don't take any chances. Shout me if you need me.'

Olivia walked up the corridor after him. Dogs flung themselves at the bars as she passed, some barking aggressively and other wagging their tails, looking like they wanted a cuddle.

'Maybe start with this one,' said Granddad, stopping outside a kennel where a fierce-looking dog was crouched in the corner. As Olivia looked in, the dog started barking – loud, staccato barks – and baring its teeth. 'Now don't you go in with it unless you're feeling confident,' said Granddad. 'This dog's been in nearly a year now and it must be getting on for eleven or twelve by my reckoning.'

'Ah, poor thing,' said Olivia. 'You can leave me to it, Granddad. I'll be careful, I promise.'

'Are you wearing your mother's amulet?' said Granddad.

'Yes, I put it on this morning when I got dressed.' Olivia fingered it under her T-shirt and felt it glow warm against her chest.

Granddad wandered a little way up the corridor, glancing back at Olivia, who was undoing the bolt and opening the kennel door. The barking inside became frantic and Olivia said in a soothing voice, 'Now what's all this about? I'm your friend. There's no need to be afraid of me.'

She stood there for a while until the barking subsided somewhat and then she took a step inside. The dog, black with a white chest, growled menacingly. Olivia ignored him, refusing to even look in his direction. She could feel him regarding her with suspicion. Eventually she decided to sit down on a ledge at the side of the kennel near the door. The dog put his head on his paws and continued to watch her. After about ten minutes she reached into her pocket for a few biscuits Granddad had given her earlier. The dog's head shot up and he growled again. 'I'm just having a little snack,' said Olivia in a low voice. 'Nothing to worry about.' She nibbled on a biscuit – plain digestive, not her favourite, but chocolate is bad for dogs and she had a plan. The dog sniffed the air. Olivia broke one of the biscuits up and placed a piece close to her feet. The dog craned his neck forward, but didn't move. Very slowly, Olivia stood up and placed another piece a little nearer to him. Still the dog didn't move, eyes glinting at her as he emitted a low grumble. He was warning her, she realized, and so sat down again. After a few more minutes she edged herself a little nearer to the dog and threw a larger fragment of biscuit so that it landed close to his feet. He backed further into the corner and snapped at her. 'That's okay,' said Olivia. 'No rush. We've all the time in the world.' She noticed scars around the dog's face, which she hadn't been able to see before. 'Oh, poor thing,' she murmured, 'no wonder you're so frightened.'

Olivia sat down again and turned her gaze away from the dog. She took her phone out of her pocket and began idly scrolling through it, not even glancing at him. She could feel him watching

her. Out of the corner of her eye, she saw him bend his neck and take the biscuit nearest to him. Not long after, he edged forward and snatched the next one, which he crunched greedily. He'd have to come really close to get another piece. Slowly he inched forward and took the biscuit gently in his mouth. Olivia became aware that she was holding her breath. She slowly released it and lifted her hand to brush a lock of hair out of her face. The dog shot back into the corner.

Olivia looked to see if there was any interesting stuff on Instagram, which she rarely bothered with these days. She became engrossed in a story by a girl she used to know back home, whose boyfriend had recently dumped her. Suddenly she felt a nudge. The dog had crept up next to her. 'Hello,' she said in a low voice. 'D'you fancy another biscuit?' Breaking one in two she put half in her mouth and held out the other half. The dog sniffed it and took it from her with gentle lips, eyeing her warily. As Olivia became absorbed in her phone again, she felt the dog pressing up to her. Slowly she reached out her hand for him to sniff and then tickled him under his chin. 'There you go, Blackie,' she said, and gave him another biscuit.

Archie's face appeared at the kennel door. 'I see it hasn't taken you long to get this one eating out of your hand,' he said. 'I'm not sure Blackie's a very original name though.' He chuckled. 'Well done, love.'

'Have you got a spare collar, Granddad? I thought Blackie might like one to make him feel special.'

'They're a few hanging up at the end. I'll get you one. Any particular colour? Leather? Gold-encrusted beads perhaps?'

'I think a plain, not very original, black one, Granddad. To match his not very original name.' Olivia put her nose in the air and sniffed. 'That will do just fine, won't it, Blackie?' She smiled as she put her arm round the dog, who looked as if he was smiling back at her.

36. Kat and Katja Overhear Nick and Felix Talking

Queenie and Duke, after a good long sleep in the kitchen, sheltering from the hot sun, were waiting outside the Big Kennels.

D'you know what a footling dandy is, Duke?' said Queenie. 'Is it another name for a Heathcliff? Or a Mr Darcy, like him in Pride and Prejudice? Me and Olivia loved that film, although not quite as much as Wuthering Heights. Either way, what's not to like? What *is* Archie's problem with Laurence?'

'Now let's see…' mused Duke.

'…Could it be that Laurence is taller than Archie?

'…Or perhaps that Laurence has got a lot more hair than Archie?

'…Or possibly that Laurence is way better-looking than Archie?

'…But I'd say the most likely explanation is that Archie's a teeny bit envious of Laurence being the Duke equivalent of the human world, bitches falling at his feet…'

'I think you mean the Valentino equivalent,

not Duke, Duke.'

'Sometimes, Queen, you can really hurt a footling dandy's feelings.'

'The footling dandy would have to have feelings to hurt,' retorted Queenie. 'Anyway, enough of footling dandies, Olivia should be out soon.'

'I hope she's all right,' said Duke. 'I don't know why she wants to bother with those dogs in there when we could be out on the Moors with Oberon.' Duke gave a long stretch and a yawn.

'Self, self, self,' said Queenie. 'Didn't you hear? She's trying to help Archie get rid of some of these dim dogs, so that he doesn't have to work as hard or provide food for them out of his own pocket. She's going to help save Kymera.'

'A worthy cause,' acknowledged Duke with a nod. 'I suppose we all have to make sacrifices and do our bit.'

Queenie couldn't decide whether he was being sincere or buttering her up or simply patronizing her. She decided to give him the benefit of the doubt. 'That's the spirit, Duke.'

'Absolutely. I expect she'll need some relaxation time now with me and Oberon.'

Duke barked excitedly as Olivia and Archie appeared at the door of the Big Kennels.

'That's a good thing you've done today, love,'

said Archie, giving her a hug. 'You're a reet grand lass.'

'I'll come and see Blackie again tomorrow and then I'll try with another one. I'd best go and see my little Kat and Katja now.'

'What about Oberon?' barked Duke.

Queenie directed an icy glare in his direction.

***

Kat

Me, Kat, here again. I'll let you into a secret. Whilst Olivia was in the Big Kennels with Archie, and Queenie and Duke were snoozing in the kitchen, I had a visitor, two visitors actually. One was that horrible Old Nick and the other nice Felix, who Mum really likes and I do too actually, except he's too much under the thumb of that nasty dad of his. They came into the Puppy Palace really quietly, like they didn't want anyone to see or hear them and they were talking in really low voices.

'I don't reckon your granddad's going to agree

to sell up,' says Nasty Nick. 'He might need a bit of persuasion.'

'Can't we just leave it, Dad? Him and Olivia really want to stay and I'd miss the place too if it went.'

'D'you want your granddad to keel over from exhaustion? Or have a heart attack or something?'

'Course not. Maybe we could…'

'It's the only way, lad. We need the place gone. Just think of the kind of life we could all have, your granddad and Olivia included. He just doesn't realize what's best for everyone. But once it's all done and dusted, he'll be grateful to us. You'll see.'

Mum's jumping up and down at the bars trying to get Felix's attention, so he opens the door and Mum runs out and leaps into his arms. 'What do you think, Katja? Do *you* want to go and live somewhere else?'

Mum listens intently, her head on one side. Her ears droop.

'Cut it out, soft lad,' says Nasty Nick. 'You're beginning to sound like Olivia, talking to the dogs as if they're hanging on your every word.'

Then Nick switches his attention to me. 'That little runt needs to go. I know someone who's very keen to get their hands on it. They'll pay a tidy sum, more than the little rat's worth.'

'Oh no, Dad. That would really upset, Olivia. She dotes on that pup.'

'Aye, perhaps you're right, son,' says Nick, patting Felix on the arm, a crafty look on his face.

'Anyway, once the other pups get sold, there might not be any need to sell Kymera. They'll bring in quite a lot, won't they, Dad?'

'Hmm,' says Nasty Nick, a glint of pure evil in his eyes as he peers down at us, 'that's true. You've given me an idea, lad.'

A shudder goes through me. Is he planning on selling us to the highest bidder, like pieces of meat? Or worse? My eyes start to glow but, remembering what Queenie said, I look away and take some deep breaths. *No magic, Kat. No magic.*

'What idea? What d'you mean?'

'Nowt, lad, nowt. Now let's get off. I meant to bring down a couple of papers for your granddad to sign. I need to go home and get them.'

'Papers? What papers?'

'Oh, I just want your granddad to witness a new will I've drawn up, that's all.'

'Well, couldn't one of us do that?'

'Oh no. You and Laurence are the main beneficiaries. That wouldn't do at all.'

Felix puts Mum down back in with us and gives her and the rest of us a pat and a stroke. 'I might just hang around to see Olivia and

Gramps.'

'Na, your mother'll be expecting us for dinner. Come on, lad. We can't keep her waiting.'

***

'Hi, babies.' Olivia bursts into the Puppy Palace, Queenie and Duke at her heels. 'Everything all right? Kat? Katja?'

'No,' we bark in unison.

'What *are* you two yapping about?' says Olivia, opening the door and picking both of us up. 'What a racket. Does this mean you're pleased to see me?'

'It's Nick and Felix. Nick's planning something awful,' I yip at her, my ears shooting up and down all by themselves.

'What's that?' barks Queenie. 'What's he planning?'

'Not you as well, Queenie,' says Olivia. 'Ssh. Granddad will be cross.'

'Shuddup, you lot,' shouts Archie from the Big Kennels. 'You're disturbing the boarders.'

'Tell me later, when we're on our own,' says Queenie quietly.

'Come on, yous,' says Olivia, cuddling me and Mum. 'Let's go out in the garden for a little play.'

37. Kat Saves the Day

Sitting down on one of the garden chairs, Olivia put Katja on the ground. 'Have a run around, Katja. You must be fed up of being cooped up with your babies.'

'Right. So what's this all about, Katja?' said Queenie immediately.

Katja began to tell her what she and Kat had overheard.

Queenie listened carefully, her eyes practically out on stalks.

'Well, the evil little sh…'

'Language, Queen,' interrupted Duke, nodding towards Kat. 'Don't want to be corrupting the young'un.'

'Since when have you ever bothered about that, Duke?' said Queenie, seething with rage.

'Only saying. You're quite happy to pull me up when I say something you don't approve of, but it's a different story…'

'Shut up, Duke,' shouted Queenie, Katja and Kat, united in angry indignation.

'Stop all the barking, you lot. What's got into you?' said Olivia, shaking her pigtails in disapproval. She ruffled little Kat's fluffy coat.

'Bark, bark, squeaky bark. I hope you're not going to turn out to be one of those awful yappy little dogs.'

Queenie Duke and Katja moved over to the corner of the garden, leaving Kat sitting on Olivia's knee, gazing longingly after them.

'D'you want to go with them?' Queenie heard Olivia say. 'Well, you can stay here and keep *me* company instead.'

Katja filled Queenie and Duke in with as much detail as she could remember.

'Hmm,' said Queenie. 'It sounds to me like Old Nick's going to try and get Archie to sign something he shouldn't be signing. We're going to have to make sure he's on the ball. He's so trusting, that's the problem.'

As if sensing that he was being talked about, Queenie saw Archie appear at the gate of the Big Kennels. It was a hot day and sweat was glistening on his brow. 'Phew,' he said, brushing his hand across his forehead, 'I'm in need of a brew. It's sweltering in those kennels. Poor dogs are sitting there panting. They're not even bothered about going out into the runs. I'll have to invest in some more fans. More expense,' he muttered, but not quietly enough to escape Queenie's sharp hearing.

'I'll make you a cuppa, Granddad,' shouted Olivia, standing up and heading for the kitchen. 'Come and sit down for a bit.'

***

Archie and Olivia were sitting cosily round the kitchen table, Queenie and the other dogs were lying around in the coolest spots they could find and Kat was perched next to Olivia on the chair, when Old Nick's head appeared at the door. 'I see, slacking, are we?' he said in an unusually jovial tone. 'This is what you get up to when I'm not about, is it?'

Queenie sat up and nodded significantly at Duke.

Archie got to his feet. 'Only popped in for a cuppa and to take the weight off for a few minutes. I'm just about to start again. No rest for the wicked, eh? Since you're here, a couple of the boarders need delivering back home. You can take the old van if you don't want them messing up your motor. And maybe you could buy a couple of those fans while you're out.'

'No problem at all,' said Nick. 'Happy to help.'

The dogs looked at him in surprise. Had the real Nick been taken over by a thoughtful alien being?

Olivia left Kat on the chair and wandered off to the bathroom and shut the door.

'Just before you go, you couldn't just sign this for us, could you, Dad?' said Nick, reaching into his back trouser pocket and bringing out some papers and a pen.

'What is it?' said Archie. 'I need to go and see to the dogs, make sure they're all all right in this heat.'

'Oh, it's just that Janey and I have updated our wills. I thought you could witness them. It won't take you a minute. Then I can drop them off at the solicitor's on my way home.'

'Aye, go on then. Where do I sign?' said Archie, sitting down again with a sigh. He picked up the papers and began fanning himself with them.

Queenie, who'd been lulled into a false sense of security by Nick being almost amiable for a change, leapt to her feet and started barking. Duke, Katja, Valentino and the other dogs joined in. Only Pookah, who was lying at Nick's feet, stayed quiet. Even Soldier added his deaf bark to the fray.

'Shuddup,' yelled Archie. 'I can't hear myself think.'

Queenie leapt on to his knee, snatched the papers out of his hand and made for the door.

Straight away, Pookah shot over and barred her way.

'What are you playing at, Queenie?' shouted Archie, as Nick bent down, seized hold of the papers and cuffed Queenie. The shock made her let go and Nick put them back in front of Archie.

'What's got into these dogs?' said Archie. 'Still, there was no need for that, Nick.'

'No. Sorry, Queenie,' said Nick, going to give her a stroke.

She bared her teeth at him.

'Okay. *Be* like that,' said Nick, handing the pen to Archie. 'There you are, Dad, just put your mark there and there.' He indicated a couple of spaces on the paper.

'Hang on a minute. Where are my specs?' said Archie. 'I can't see a thing without them. Not close to at any rate.'

'You don't need your specs to sign your name,' said Nick. 'Just a quick scribble, and then I'll come with you into the kennels and pick up those dogs.'

'Aye, okay,' said Archie, bending over the paper and screwing up his eyes. 'Where do I need to sign again?'

'Somebody *do* something,' barked Queenie. 'Duke, Kat, Katja.'

Next minute there was an almighty screech

from outside.

Archie leapt to his feet.

Olivia came rushing out of the bathroom.

They both ran into the garden, dogs and Nick behind them, to find Kat floundering in the duck pond, squealing her little head off.

'Oh my God,' said Olivia, running over and grabbing her by the scruff and hauling her out. 'How did you get in there? Was nobody watching her?' She turned to look accusingly at Archie and Nick.

'Don't be blaming other people, Olivia. It's your job to look after your own dog,' snapped Archie. 'That's one lucky pup. A minute or two later and it could have been a very different story.'

Olivia burst into tears as Archie headed towards the Big Kennels.

'Er. What about the papers?' Nick shouted after him.

'It'll have to do another day,' said Archie. 'I've work to do.'

My Thirteenth Birthday

I couldn't wait for school to finish that day, for you to come and pick me up and show me the surprise I'd heard you whispering about the night before. She'll love it, you said. We'll give it her when she comes home from school. I'd have liked her to have one of Dad's, but she doesn't want to wait and none of his are due in season for a while, he says. She wants one now and she's old enough to look after one. Our little girl's going to be a teenager, Max, all grown up. I can't wait to see her face.

I can still see the prefect, the bossy one with frizzy red hair, interrupting the geography lesson, telling the teacher that the headmistress wanted to speak to me. Maybe I was going to be allowed to leave school early because it was my birthday? After all, it was a kind of landmark. When you become a teenager, that's when real life starts. That's what you always said, Mum.

As we walked over to the office, I asked the prefect why the head wanted to see me. She just shrugged and didn't answer. Maybe she didn't know, or maybe she didn't want to be the one to tell me.

I'd always found the head rather intimidating -

stern and formidable - but she stood up as I entered the inner sanctum, like I was royalty or something. She looked anxious and kindly rather than severe. She took hold of my hand, led me to a chair, and pulled up one next to me. She began speaking in a low, soft voice, all the while keeping hold of my hand. I remember focusing on the toothpaste mark on the lapel of her pale blue suit, wondering whether to tell her about it in case she didn't know, anything not to hear the words coming out of her mouth. The lorry was out of control. They think the driver may have had a heart attack. They didn't stand a chance. It was nobody's fault. I'm so sorry, Olivia. They wouldn't have suffered. Death would have been instantaneous. STOP SAYING THOSE THINGS, I wanted to yell at her. IT'S NOT TRUE. IT CAN'T BE TRUE. I must be having a nightmare. I want to wake up. NOW.

Only I never did, Mum. The wish I made on my seventh birthday – Please, oh please, let me live at Kymera - came true instead. Granddad's words go round and round in my head:

Be careful what you wish for, Olivia...

38. The Moors

'I think it's time I took those dogs out, Granddad.'

'Dogs? What dogs?' Archie was munching on a jam and cheese butty Olivia had made for him and reading the paper, his specs propped on the end of his nose. The sun was beating down in the garden and Archie had erected a makeshift parasol out of an old sheet and some slats of wood to keep off the fiercest of its scorching rays.

'The ex-vicious dogs, *those* dogs.'

Archie looked up. 'You've done a grand job with those dogs, love. One by one you've brought them round. I don't think anybody else could have done that. But do you think they're ready to go out? Remember, they've not been in the outside world for months, years, some of them.'

'Then it's time they did,' said Olivia decisively. 'I'll take them today, later on when it's cooled down a bit. We're not likely to bump into anyone on the Moors, maybe the odd rider, but that's all. I'll take Queenie and Duke and Val, in fact all our dogs, and I'll carry Kat.'

'I'd leave Old Soldier behind if I were you, he's bound to slow you up.'

'I think Soldier would like to come too. He's

probably not left the place in ages. I won't take Oberon this time though.'

'I should jolly well think not,' said Archie. 'I don't know – dogs, horses, strays, you'll be after taking a goat along next.'

It was getting on for five in the afternoon when Archie decided it was cool enough to take the dogs out. 'I'll go get them for you. D'you want them on leads? They might run off, you know. First taste of freedom.'

'I'll take a couple of leads with me,' said Olivia, 'just in case. But I think I'll let them run free.'

'Remember to have them back in time for their teas,' said Archie as he stood up to go and fetch them. 'I'll feed them a little later today.'

Olivia got changed into an old pair of jeans and a T-shirt and put on her walking shoes. Not that they'd be walking very far this time. Best to see how it went first. She wasn't worried though, more excited that the dogs would finally start to have something of a life. It didn't even occur to her that they'd run into any trouble.

***

KAT

I'm excited too. Even if I am going to be carried instead of running with the others. At least I'm getting out and about and seeing a bit of the world. There's Archie now, bringing out the ex-vicious dogs. They look very shy, not vicious at all, sticking close to Archie's legs. It's like they can't believe it when he opens the gate to let them out.

'Come on, Blackie, Whitey, Brownie, Bluey,' calls Olivia.

Blimey, Kat doesn't seem such a bad name after all.

They run to her and cosy around her legs and she bends down to stroke them with her free hand. 'This is Kat,' she tells them, showing me to them, but they don't seem terribly interested. They obviously don't know how important I am in Dogsworld. They all look pretty much alike, apart from being different colours, with ugly faces covered in marks and funny sticky-up ears. I feel a bit sorry for them. None of them have got proper tails either, but they wag their stumps shyly. It's like their whole bottoms are wagging.

'Okay, everybody, are we ready? Duke, Valentino, Queenie, Queenie Two, Soldier, come on, we're off out.'

Queenie's hanging back and looking like she might want to stay with Archie. 'You *are* coming with us, aren't you, Queenie?' I yip at her.

'You go with them, Queenie, it'll do you good,' says Archie. 'Call her, Olivia.'

'Come on, Queenie, we won't be long, I need you to keep the rabble under control.'

Valentino's not looking too happy either, eyeing up the other dogs, who do have rather fierce faces, I must say.

Duke's just bounding about as usual, ignoring everybody except Olivia.

Eventually we all set off. I'm glad Queenie's coming with us. I feel safer when she's around. The new dogs stay close to Olivia and keep looking round like they can't believe they're out.

What a wonderful place 'The Moors' is. Green fields stretch before us, with little paths, bridle paths Olivia calls them, running through them. 'Are we all having a good time?' says Olivia. I'm speechless. I haven't a yip in me. I never knew such a marvel could exist. No wonder Duke is always so keen to go out with Olivia and Oberon.

We set off down a long path with dykes on

both sides. Duke soon goes off and does his own thing, leaping one of the dykes into the next field and giving chase to a rabbit he's spotted nibbling some grass. Watching that little tail bobbing about in the grass as the rabbit shoots off with Duke close on its tail, I want to go with him. I struggle in Olivia's arms.

'Stop it, Kat,' she says, laughing. 'You can't go chasing rabbits. You'll just have to watch for now. You're too young to go gallivanting yet. I may let you down for a few minutes when we're nearly back.'

I look down at the other dogs. They seem happy just to sniff around at the sides of the dykes, doing little wees and eating the odd dollop of horse muck. Duke seems to be having a much better time than anybody else. When will I be old enough to go with him? I heard Archie telling Bob the other day that me and my sisters were nearly six weeks old, so I'm sure it can't be long now.

In the distance, heading in our direction, I can see a long line of horses, like Oberon. I like Oberon. It will be nice to make the acquaintance of some other horses. Suddenly though, they start to run, galloping I think it's called. They're rushing towards us very quickly.

'Whoops,' says Olivia. 'I don't like the look

of this. Get over to the side, you lot. Quickly! Get here, now. Soldier, Queenie Two, Valentino, Blackie…'

The dogs don't seem to have a clue, dawdling around in the middle of the path. Lucky there's Queenie. She shoots over to them and noses them to the side, and only just in time too. The horse in front is nearly upon us and, catching sight of all the dogs, gives a massive leap in the opposite direction, only just missing the dyke. The girl sitting on its back shoots up in the air and lands at our feet with a bump. Ouch. The other horses manage to stop a short distance from us. The horse that nearly fell into the dyke stands trembling next to the girl on the ground, snorting and snuffling, its white coat all gleaming with sweat.

'Are you all right?' says Olivia in a worried voice, holding out her hand to help the girl to her feet. 'Are you hurt?'

'I don't think so,' says the girl in a shaky voice. 'I'm awfully sorry about that. This black and white dog suddenly shot in front of us and frightened the horses. I think it was chasing a rabbit. It all happened so quickly. People shouldn't be allowed to have dogs unless they can keep them under control. I mean, look at all yours, they're perfectly behaved.'

'That'll be Duke,' I bark.

'Quiet,' barks Queenie.

'Perhaps it was a stray,' says Olivia quickly. 'Well, we'd better get on. I'm glad you're okay. Come on, dogs.'

The dogs walk quietly past the line of horses, some of whom look as if they're dancing. I don't know why Olivia didn't tell the girl that it was Duke who'd been chasing the rabbit.

'Move along, dogs, quickly now,' barks Queenie, nudging them to walk faster. Soldier refuses to be rushed and ambles along at his own pace, which is hardly moving at all. We keep having to wait for him, but Olivia keeps giving him a stroke and telling him how clever he is. He doesn't seem awfully clever to me, but *she* knows best. I'm just glad I wasn't on the ground when those horses came rushing up or I might have been trampled on. Perhaps it's better to be carried after all.

39. A Dog Runs Off

Kat

There's a bridge at the end of the path that crosses over the sluice, which is much wider than the dykes and runs for miles and miles, so Olivia tells me and the other dogs. We turn right over the bridge and there, swimming in the sluice, is Duke, cooling down after chasing the rabbit he didn't catch. Queenie says he never catches them.

'You're a naughty dog, Duke. You could have caused an accident there,' Olivia shouts at him. I've never heard her shout at Duke before. He clambers out and shakes himself, water flying everywhere, making everybody nearly as wet as himself. He doesn't look at all sorry. In fact he looks very pleased with himself, wagging his tail lots as if he's done something really clever. I think I'd feel the same.

'You'll get us all into trouble if you're not careful, Duke,' says Olivia, wagging a finger at him. She doesn't sound terribly cross, but Queenie's looking really mad.

'They could report you for that, Duke,' she says. 'Don't you ever think of anybody…?'

But Duke's shot off again after another rabbit even before Queenie's finished speaking. I think she'll have something to say about that later. It does seem rather rude after all.

Olivia calls after him – 'Duke, Duke!' - but he takes no notice. I give her face a lick to show her that *I* understand at least.

'You're a good girl, Kat,' she says. 'I hope you won't grow up to be as disobedient as Duke. I'll give him a proper talking-to when we get back.'

'You won't be the only one,' barks Queenie.

Olivia points to a house in the distance on the edge of a road. 'That's where Uncle Nick lives,' she says, 'and where Granddad used to live.' She shrugs. 'I've only been there once, when Felix was living at home. Auntie Janey gave me a fairy cake and a cup of tea. She was nice, too nice for Uncle Nick.'

We carry on walking, down one path and up another. Olivia's chattering away to the dogs with colours for names, telling them how good they are, when the one called Blackie takes off in the wrong direction and won't come when she shouts after him. 'Oh, dear,' says Olivia, as she watches him getting smaller and smaller in the distance. 'I hope he'll be all right. D'you think he'll be able to find his way back?' The other three stick close to Olivia's legs, but don't answer her of course. I've a funny feeling he won't.

Even if I can't run with Duke yet, I'd love to walk with the others and sniff about like them and roll on my back from side to side and kick my feet in the air. It looks great fun. They all seem to take it in turns to roll in the same place instead of finding their own spots. Even Queenie joins in with the rolling business, so it must not only be fun, but quite sensible too.

To get back to Kymera, we have to jump a small dyke and walk through a field. Everybody manages that without any trouble, except for Soldier, who just stands there looking a bit stupid. Nobody except me seems to notice he's been left behind. Just as I'm wondering what to do about it, he starts barking loudly. Everybody turns round to look at him. His big eyes look really sad, as if he's about to start crying, and he shakes his head, his long floppy ears waving from side to side.

'Come on, Soldier, you can do it, you've done it lots of times before,' shouts Olivia. But Soldier doesn't move, looking like a gormless gobbin, something Archie says to Olivia when she's staring into space. It makes her laugh.

'Go back for him, will you, Queenie,' says Olivia. Queenie's in the lead, probably wanting to get back to Archie and looks a bit annoyed, as if she can hardly be bothered.

'Just leave him,' she barks, looking towards Kymera with a worried expression. 'He knows where he lives.'

'Go on, Queenie, I'm tired,' says Olivia. 'You know what a dope he is. He'll never find his own way home. We can't just leave him.'

As Queenie turns back to fetch Soldier, Duke appears in the distance. He soon reaches the dyke, stops behind Soldier and gives his back legs a nudge. Soldier, Granddad, I suppose I should call him really, still doesn't budge and carries on barking loudly. I'm tempted to try whizzing him over myself, except I think that might make Queenie cross, but then Duke gives him a little nip on one of his legs. With a yelp, Soldier shoots forward over the dyke and slowly pads up to join the rest of us.

Neat trick, Duke. Obviously no magic involved or Queenie would have given him a rollicking.

'About time, Duke. Where've you been?' says Queenie sharply.

'Actually, Queen, I saw that daft dog run off and I chased after it. I couldn't catch it though. It looked like it was running for its life.'

'Hmm,' says Queenie. 'Just don't be causing

any more trouble.'

Olivia puts me down so that I can play in the long grass for a few minutes. I jump about and pretend to chase rabbits like Duke. It's great fun, but it doesn't last long. Olivia picks me up again. 'Did you enjoy that, Kat?' she says, giving me a cuddle. I nod and my right ear shoots up in the air. Olivia laughs and we head for home.

***

Back at Kymera, Archie's standing waiting for us at the edge of the back field. 'How did it go, love? Any problems?'

'Blackie ran off,' says Olivia. 'I'm really sorry, Granddad. And Duke frightened some horses and they bolted.'

'Oh heck,' says Archie. 'That Blackie one will probably turn up in his own time once he's had a taste of freedom. Don't be worrying too much. What happened with the horses? Did they know it was our Duke?'

'No,' says Olivia, going red. 'I pretended he wasn't with us.'

'Well done, love. We don't need any more bother. Nobody was hurt, were they?'

'One girl fell off, but she seemed okay. I think they were from that riding school. I never usually see anybody on the Moors. They *would* be there today when I had all the dogs with me.'

'Let's just hope they don't put in a complaint,' says Archie. 'Anyway, I'll get these three back inside. Come on, Whitey, Bluey, Brownie, whatever you're called, let's be having you. It's tea-time.'

Olivia gives them all a stroke and tells them they've been very good. They follow Archie into the Big Kennels quite happily. Probably thinking of their teas, certainly not about Blackie. I can tell Olivia is though. Her face is all sad. I think he was probably her favourite of the four and she won't like thinking of him out there on his own.

40. Laurence Brings Some News

Blackie didn't come back that night and so, early next morning, Olivia decided to take Oberon out on the Moors to see if they could spot him anywhere. She wandered round to the stables, Duke barking excitedly by her side.

'I don't know if you should come with us, Duke, after the trouble you've caused. Maybe you should just stay here.'

Duke's tail drooped as he turned beseeching eyes on Olivia.

'Oh, all right then,' she relented, 'but you'd better be good.'

Duke sat next to the stable door and never uttered a sound, like he'd heard and taken on board what she'd said.

Oberon stood by munching grass as Olivia mucked out the stable before their ride. She didn't mind the mucking out. In fact she didn't even mind picking up the horse muck with her bare hands, although she generally used a fork and shovel. And she loved the smell of clean straw and hay. As she brushed out the stable, she wondered why Blackie had run off like that. Probably, as

Granddad said, his first taste of freedom. Who knew what went on in his mind? Hopefully he'd come back soon, or she'd come across him on the Moors and persuade him to follow them home.

Oberon stood quite still as Olivia groomed him, brushing his coat until it shone and combing out any tangles in his mane and tail. He seemed to understand her mood and, every now and then, he put his nose up to her and nudged her gently. He always stood patiently as she picked out his feet. 'We'll have to get the blacksmith to call soon, Oberon,' she said. 'Granddad won't like that. I'll need to get a paper round to pay for these things.'

Oberon neighed like he was agreeing with her and nodded his head several times.

Duke barked impatiently.

'All right, Duke,' said Olivia. 'We're nearly ready. But you're on a warning. Remember, no upsetting anybody today.'

Duke looked rather subdued as Olivia got on with the business of tacking up Oberon.

'Come on, then, you,' said Olivia. 'But stick with me. No running off by yourself. Keep an eye out for Blackie.'

Duke barked enthusiastically. He was never quiet for very long.

Olivia was disappointed. They hadn't even caught a glimpse of Blackie during their ride. She felt cheered up though when she caught sight of Laurence's jag in the driveway on their return. She wouldn't have time to check herself over before she saw him, not unless she sneaked past him. He'd probably be sitting in the garden. But anyway, she looked quite smart in her riding gear. Her jodhpurs clung to her, emphasizing her slim figure and she was wearing her purple 'I Love Dogs' T-shirt. Once she'd untacked Oberon and given him a couple of mints and a hug before letting him loose in the field, she shook out her hair and strode confidently towards the Manor.

'There you are, Liv,' said Laurence, standing up as she approached. 'I was beginning to think I'd have to leave without seeing you.' He pulled her close and gave her a hug. 'You smell all nice and horsey…' he said, nuzzling her hair, '…and you look great in that gear, all grown up.'

Olivia felt herself go red – why did she always do that? – as her heart began to beat faster. Laurence looked gorgeous as usual, his jet-black hair curling round his shoulders. He was dressed more casually today, in jeans and a white T-shirt, which emphasized his tan. How could anybody be *that* good-looking?

'Isn't Felix with you?'

'No, I left him at home arguing with Dad.'

'Felix arguing? I've never known Felix argue with anybody, especially not his dad.'

'Maybe there's quite a lot you don't know about Felix.'

Olivia stared at Laurence. 'What's that supposed to mean?'

'No, nothing. Forget I said anything. I've brought Pookah back and I didn't want to disturb Granddad and you weren't about, so I made myself a pot of tea. Shall I pour you a cup? I've only just made it. How was your ride?'

'I was looking for Blackie.'

'Blackie? Who's Blackie?'

Olivia explained about the ex-fighting dogs and what had taken place the previous day.

Laurence listened and nodded. 'I'm sorry that happened after all your hard work, Liv. And, as for you, Duke, you *have* been a naughty lad, haven't you?' Laurence bent down and gave Duke a stroke. '*I* don't know. What *are* we going to do with you?'

He turned back to Olivia. 'I shouldn't worry too much, Liv. He'll probably turn up in his own time. These dogs have a homing instinct.' He laid his hand on top of Olivia's and gave it a comforting squeeze.

'What are you doing here again so soon,

young Laurence?' Granddad emerged from the Big Kennels, not looking very happy to see him cosying up to Olivia.

Olivia surreptitiously slid her hand away from under Laurence's as Granddad pulled up a chair. 'Is there any tea left in that pot?'

'Sure, Granddad. I made enough for us all. I've brought Pookah back. She turned up at ours. Clever dog, eh? Finding her way home? Nearly as clever as your Queenie.'

Queenie, who was sitting under the table, gave a series of little barks. Pookah glared at everybody from near the pond, her pink eyes glittering.

'I don't think Queenie agrees with you there,' said Archie. 'So, what else is new?'

'Nana Sylvia showed up at ours last night.'

'Nana Sylvia? You've seen your grandmother?' said Archie with a sharp intake of breath. 'I didn't know *she* was back on the scene.'

'She called round to see Dad. I hardly recognised her, it's been so long. I was only a kid when I last saw her. She was asking after Liv.'

'*I* don't want to see her,' said Olivia, shaking her head. 'Not after the way she treated Granddad. And Mum,' she added in a low voice. 'Anyway, I'm going to go and get Kat out. She's probably missed me.' Olivia marched off, feeling cross and out of sorts. Nana Sylvia indeed. Mum didn't even like her name being mentioned. She refused to talk about 'my so-called mother'. Olivia had never even met her.

As she came back with Kat in her arms, she heard Granddad say, 'Why is *she* sniffing around anyway? She must be after something.'

'She was just asking after everybody and about this place, how it was doing. And she asked about *you*, Granddad.'

'Pfft. She should crawl back under whatever stone she's crawled out from,' said Granddad, frowning.

'Dad seemed pleased to see her anyway. She was quite a laugh actually.' Laurence shrugged.

Olivia said nothing as she stroked Kat's fluffy coat and played with her ears.

'Your father always *was* soft in the head where she was concerned. You watch yourself with *her*, lad. She can smell trouble from miles away. She's like a fox with the scent of a rabbit. She's not back living round here, is she?'

'She's come to look after her mother, who's not so good, she told Dad.'

'Not the mythical Beattie?' said Archie scornfully. 'The mother who never even turned up to see her daughter wed? I always thought she was a figment of Sylvia's imagination. Do you know that all the time we were together, she never visited. Not once. Never laid eyes on her. There was always some reason why she stayed away: she suffered from "social anxiety", whatever *that* is when it's at home - some made-up complaint; or she'd come down with a mysterious illness; or she'd been inexplicably called away.' Archie snorted in disgust and banged his hand down on the table. 'I gave up bothering in the end. Didn't think she'd still be alive. Don't tell me you've finally met your great-grandma? You've done better than me if you have.'

Laurence shook his head. 'No, it was only Nana Sylvia, on a flying visit; she didn't bring the old lady.'

'Come to look after her mother indeed.' Archie gave another snort. 'Sylvia's never looked after anybody in her life except Sylvia. There'll be something in it for *her,* you mark my words. Don't you be bringing her down here to see Olivia. D'you hear?'

'No,' said Olivia. 'I deffo don't want to see her. Ever.'

'Hey. Don't shoot the messenger,' said Laurence, holding both hands in the air as he stood up. 'Anyway, I'd best go. Stuff to do, you know.'

Olivia carried the pup round to the drive to see Laurence off, Archie and the dogs following in their wake. 'You'll call again soon, Laurence, won't you?'

'You know me, the proverbial bad penny,' said Laurence, giving her a conspiratorial wink and a wave and leaping into his car. Olivia gazed after him as he drove off, a strange, unsettling feeling filling her chest.

41. Queenie's Tale

Queenie

'Who's Sylvia, Queenie?' said Kat.

Olivia had left the dogs on their own in the kitchen, after making sure that Pookah wasn't anywhere around, while she went to check up on the ex-fighting dogs in the Big Kennels. 'Look after Kat whilst I'm gone,' she'd instructed Queenie and Duke. 'And don't be getting up to any mischief, any of you.'

'Don't talk to me about that Sylvia,' snapped Queenie. 'A bitch and a half, that one.'

'Yes, but who is she?' insisted Kat, ears flapping up and down with a will of their own.

'Archie's wife, ex-wife, I should say.'

Kat's eyes became round like saucers. 'I didn't know Archie had been married, Queenie.'

'Oh yes, he was married all right. I first met Sylvia when Archie took me to live with him after my first human got arrested.'

'Arrested?' repeated Kat, jumping up and down on the spot.

'That's what I said. Now he was called…'

'We're not having this old story again, are we, Queen?' interrupted Duke.

'Shut up, Duke,' said Queenie and Kat at the same time.

'Well, can you make it the short version?' said Duke, curling up into a ball and shutting his eyes.

'As I was saying,' continued Queenie, 'before I was so rudely interrupted, I used to live with a jolly chap called Tipsy Tim, not a bad sort of fella deep down. We used to go to the pub together and he'd buy himself a pint and one for me. I could only manage the one, not being a big drinker, but he'd down three or four.

'On the way home this particular night, young Tim, who'd supped a good five pints, fell asleep in the car at the traffic lights. I was in the back with my pups, Queenie Two amongst them. Well, Tim got carted off in a police van and two policemen tried to get a hold of me. Obviously, I wasn't going to let a couple of strangers come anywhere near, not when I had babies to look after. That's when they rang Archie, but I wasn't any happier about seeing him to be honest. Tried to bite him straight off.'

'Bite him, Queenie? You tried to bite Archie?' said Kat looking shocked.

'I didn't know him, remember. Anyway, he

was terrified. Went to Kymera for a pair of strong gloves and this net thingy. I put up a good fight, but he finally managed to get me all tangled up in the net and took me back to his house with the pups.

'I soon found I rather liked living in a proper house with proper food and a proper bed with blankets, and I was growing quite a bit fond of Archie. Not of Sylvia though, his other half. What a nasty piece of work *she* was. Kept yelling, "Get that filthy mutt and its disgusting offspring out of my house. Take them down to those manky kennels you're so fond of." But Archie refused to ship us off.'

Kat stared at Queenie with a shocked expression. 'Didn't Tipsy Tim want you back, Queenie?'

'Oh, he wanted me back all right. He went to prison for a few months and when they let him out, he came looking for me. Archie wouldn't let me go, said he'd grown attached. There was some argy-bargy between the two of them and Archie ended up paying quite a lot of money for me, at least one hundred pounds.'

Queenie looked around at her spellbound audience. Even Valentino was sitting to attention, his tail motionless for once.

Duke gave a loud snore.

Kat's ears were practically taking off.

'Anyway, kindly let me finish without interruption,' said Queenie. 'One night, there was a right blazing row between Archie and Sylvia. I even heard *my* name being bandied about. The pups were shivering in their bed and I had to cover my delicate ears with my paws. The language! Then the bitch turfed us all out into the night, Archie and all.'

'This ain't the short version,' said Duke, lifting his head.

'Please be quiet when I'm speaking, Duke. It turned out to be the end of the high life for me. We had to come and live in Archie's caravan on Kymera. A proper comedown it was, what with only one blanket to share between us. I tell you, Kat, Valentino, Tipsy Tim's place was a palace compared to that caravan. Archie used to have to wee on the lock to unfreeze it before he could open it on a cold winter's morning. Sometimes it took so long, he'd ask for my contribution. "Come on, Queenie," he'd say, picking me up and aiming my bottom at the door, "we're going to be stuck in here all day at this rate. Give us a jimmy riddle." It didn't bother me. I was more than happy to oblige.'

'Yes, I remember the pong in that caravan,' said Duke, grimacing. 'I was too polite to mention it at the time. I never actually met that Sylvia though.'

'Think yourself lucky, Duke. And it wasn't even Archie's first attempt at living happily ever after with Sylvia. First time round, according to him, he arrived home from work to find the kids locked in the broom cupboard, Nick screaming to be let out and little Jess, Olivia's mum, sobbing her heart out, whilst their mother sat drinking in the kitchen with a strange man. Archie reckons he sent her packing with her tail between her legs, but there are those that say he came home, hoping to find his tea on the table, but found a goodbye note from Sylvia instead.'

'No,' said Kat, eyes wider than ever. 'Poor Jess. I even feel a bit sorry for Nick. No wonder Olivia doesn't want anything to do with that horrid woman.'

'Exactly.' Queenie nodded. 'At least she had the good grace to leave with nothing that first time. Then again, that was probably because half of nothing *is* nothing.

'Years later Archie bumped into her in a pub somewhere. She made out she missed him and the kids. Said it had all been a terrible mistake. So the great lummox moved her into the house he'd worked so hard for. The kids were teenagers by then. Nick was thrilled, even though she'd been such a rotten mother. Not Jessica though. *She* was a real daddy's girl.

'Sylvia hadn't really changed. She still gave Archie a dog's life, always shouting and tossing her splendid locks in temper, wild and tempestuous. She had a fine head of hair, I'll give her that, the only good thing I can say about her. Nick eventually took up with Janey and Jess moved out as soon as she was old enough and it was just the two of them left, Archie and Sylvia.

'And then, after the row, it was just Archie and me. Archie paid Sylvia off with a wad of cash, leaving him virtually penniless. You only have to look at my balding, soft old coot to know that he'd give his last penny away to help somebody. "I can't let Sylvia go short, Queenie," the daft beggar said. No, but it was all right for me and him to huddle together for warmth in a single bed in that freezing caravan. He must have known that Sylvia wouldn't "go short" if she were surrounded by a horde of starving, motherless pups. The last morsel would still go straight down *her* throat.'

Kat gasped in disbelief. 'Poor Archie. What a nasty, nasty person that Sylvia must be.'

'He could learn a thing or two from us dogs, could Archie,' said Queenie. 'I mean, you don't see Duke with a string of exes clamouring for his last bone – "Pleez, Duke, I am nothing vithout you. I vill die of bone deprivation." Na. Live in the moment and move on. No regrets. No recriminations. That's the dog way.'

'You making fun of me, Queen?' said Duke, sitting up.

'Quiet, please,' said Queenie, turning her back on him. 'So Sylvia left, probably to find herself another mug. And, instead of moving us back into the house, Archie went and gave it to Nick, who was lodging in a mobile home in the back garden with Janey and the two lads.

'Not only that, he gave Nick a half share in Kymera, hoping for a helping hand with things now that he'd clocked up several hundred dog years. But all Nick has ever done is help himself to the money, not that there's much money to help himself to anymore.

'After a few months, Nick offered Archie the mobile home which he and Janey wanted rid of. It was little more than a dilapidated shack by then, cluttering up their back garden. A house in exchange for a glorified caravan? Fair swap, Archie.

'But Archie's a "glass half full" kind of chap and he got one of his builder chums to pick it up the very next day and build a brick base for it to stand on. "We'll call it Ky Manor. What d'you reckon, Queenie?" he said.

'I must admit, I rather liked the idea of saying to my mates, "Hey, I live at Ky Manor." Let them think: *Wow, drawing room, servants, oak beams, gatehouse*. No need to mention *rickety cabin, ice on the inside of the windows in winter, coats piled on the bed for warmth, radiators that rattle and creak but never manage to warm up*.

'At least it's a step up from the caravan and young Olivia doesn't have to sleep with a peg on her nose. It's not what the girl's used to or deserves. It may not be posh, or even entirely weather-proof, but it's home, especially now Archie's built on an extra room and a porch and installed a primitive central heating system, even if it hardly ever works. Still, we've got the log fire, which makes it lovely and cosy in winter and the wooden veranda at the back is grand for us dogs to sit out in the warmer weather.

And we're happy.'

42. Archie's Version

'What are you dogs up to?' said Olivia, coming into the kitchen, followed by Archie. 'Look at Queenie, Granddad. She looks like she's holding court.'

'Why d'you think she's called Queenie?' said Archie. 'She's always thought herself a cut above. Thinks she's better than the rest of the dogs, likes to rule the roost. It's her upbringing. She had a tough start in life, practically had to fend for herself. Queenie seemed like a good name for her. I've always been good at picking names for the dogs.'

'Hmm,' said Olivia. 'Haven't you had her from a pup then, Granddad?'

'If you make us a nice cuppa, I'll tell you how she came to live with me. Get the kettle on, there's a good lass.'

Olivia put the kettle on and Granddad settled himself down at the kitchen table. Olivia poured the tea, picked up Kat and sat down to join him.

'So,' said Archie, 'there I was, sitting comfortably at home, that's the house I shared with Sylvia, your so-called grandmother - where Nick lives now - watching the telly, minding my own business, when the phone rings and it's the local constabulary. "Sorry to bother you, Mr. Truelove," they say, "but we've got a young dog here and we can't do nothing with it. It's snapping and snarling and nearly had us hands off when we tried to get hold of it. We've arrested its owner for driving whilst under the influence and the dog's in the back of the car with some pups. We'd really appreciate your help, what with you being such an expert. We didn't know who else to call."

'Well, what could I do? Sylvia told me to let them deal with it themselves, but you can't ignore a cry for help. So, I went along, and Queenie – who didn't have a name at the time, the young fella who owned her, Tipsy Tim he was known as, just used to call her "dog" – was guarding a litter of pups, giving the two policemen a heck of a time, trying to bite them.

'"Come here, you," I said, and she came straight to me. Like putty in my hands, she was. The two police officers stood there gawping. Couldn't believe their eyes. I took Queenie home, along with her pups, one of whom was Queenie Two here. Sylvia, well, she didn't like it, to put it mildly. She wasn't what you might call a dog-lover. She made such a hoo-ha that I decided me and Queenie and the pups should move out and that's when we came to live at Kymera, in a smart little caravan. It was before we had the Manor. I often used to stay over in the caravan after I'd finished my chores here anyway, what with Sylvia not being the easiest person to get along with. And the rest, as they say, is history. It was just me and Queenie from then on.'

'Wow. Really? And haven't you seen Sylvia since?'

'Not heard a peep from her. Nor do I want to.'

'What about that Tim? Did he not want Queenie back?'

'Once they let him out of clink, he came looking for her, but Queenie had made up her mind she was stopping with me. I wouldn't say young Tim ill-treated her exactly, but he wasn't really capable of looking after a dog, not the way he used to drink. He even gave our Queenie a taste for beer. Anyway, she went for him when he turned up here, gave him a right sharp nip.'

'No! She bit him?'

'She did. I had to give him a couple of quid to go away even though, by rights, he should have been paying *me* for her board whilst he was in custody.'

A loud snoring noise floated up from under the table.

'You must have tired Duke out,' said Archie.

'He's dead to the world.'

'All the dogs seem tired, Granddad,' said Olivia, looking round at them. Kat was dozing on her lap. Valentino was stretched out on the moth-eaten chair, feet twitching. Soldier was comatose behind the cooker. Even Queenie Two had stopped her usual scavenging and was flat out next to Duke.

Only Queenie was still alert, staring intently at Archie.

'At least Queenie's still awake,' said Olivia. 'She doesn't seem as tired as the others.'

'Lazy lot,' said Archie, getting up. 'I'm going to make myself a butty. D'you fancy one, love?'

'No thanks. I'm not really hungry. That was a good story, Granddad,' said Olivia, bending down to give Queenie a stroke. 'And fancy you being such a fierce dog, Queenie.'

***

'Granddad?' said Olivia, casually stroking Kat's fluffy coat as they watched Archie tucking into his sandwich.

'Yes, love?'

'Is Kymera worth a lot of money? Is that why Uncle Nick wants to sell? I mean, no offence, but it seems quite run-down to me.'

'It's not the place itself. It's the land. There are those that want it to build on. You could get a lot of houses on Kymera, which the builders could sell for a fortune.'

'D'you think that's why Sylvia's suddenly come back? D'you think she's in cahoots with Uncle Nick?'

'I must admit, that had crossed my mind,' said Archie, taking a sip of his tea. 'Still, nobody can do anything without my say-so and there's no way I'm selling up. There's plenty of places that could be built on without spoiling our bit of countryside. This place belonged to my dad, you know, Olivia. He'd be turning in his grave if he thought it was going to be sold to make some shysters rich. And, apart from all that, we have lots of birds nesting here that are dwindling in this country and they need preserving. They're part of our heritage.'

Olivia stood up and began to wash some pots with one hand in the kitchen sink, still holding on to Kat with the other. Kat had woken up and was looking at Olivia with worried eyes. 'I'm going to help you more, Granddad. We'll make Kymera work. Tomorrow I'm going to start by doing some painting, spruce the place up a bit.'

Archie stood up and ruffled her hair. 'You're a grand lass, Olivia, but I'm not sure a spot of paint is going to do the trick. Maybe when these pups are sold, we can start to get out of this hole I seem to have got us in.'

'It's not your fault, Granddad. You work yourself to the bone. It's Uncle Nick who should be doing more. I might have a word with Laurence and Felix. We all need to pull our weight.'

Little Kat started yipping and one ear flew up in the air.

'See,' said Olivia. 'Kat approves.'

Archie laughed. 'Well that's the main thing. Perhaps she could tell us how to make a bit more money. Anyway, back to the boarders. You can come and help me feed in about an hour if you like.'

43. The Dog Inspector

It was the first gloomy day in ages. The sun struggled to show its face and the rain kept falling and stopping and then falling again. In the kitchen, Queenie was chatting to Duke, who was looking bored, about disobedient dogs who ran after rabbits and put horses and riders in danger. Valentino was wagging his tail, giving the impression that he was following the conversation with interest, although he probably wasn't. Queenie Two was snuffling about looking for scraps of food. And Soldier was asleep behind the cooker.

'I'm worried about Blackie, Kat,' said Olivia, who was sitting at the kitchen table, messing with her phone. Kat, who was perched on her knee, looked up at her and nodded. 'It's been three days since he went missing. I feel awful, like it's my fault.'

'It's not your fault. You were trying to do a good thing,' yipped Kat, popping her ears up and down and fluffing out her woolly coat.

'Well said, Kat,' said Queenie, coming out from under the table. 'Don't blame yourself, Olivia,' she barked.

Duke came and nuzzled Olivia's hand.

Valentino barked randomly.

Queenie Two carried on snuffling for food.

'Ah, thanks, dogs. I don't know what you're saying, but it helps anyway. I'm just not sure what to do next. Maybe I'll just make some 'Missing' posters or put something on Facebook.'

There was a rap on the kitchen door, which made them all jump. 'Hello, anybody there?'

Olivia jumped up and opened the door. A young man was standing there with an umbrella and a clipboard.

'Ah, you're in,' he said. 'Is the boss at home?'

'He's cleaning out the Big Kennels,' said Olivia.

'Well, I need to speak to him on a matter of some urgency.'

'Who are you?' said Olivia.

'I'm the Dog Inspector, young lady,' said the man, assuming an 'I'm a very important person' expression. 'I represent the RSPCA. Now kindly fetch the boss.'

'All right. Have a seat,' said Olivia, indicating one of the not-so-new chairs at the table.

The man sniffed, folded up his umbrella, took out a hanky from his top pocket and brushed the seat with it before gingerly lowering himself down.

As soon as Olivia had left the room, Kat in her arms, the man stood up and began poking around, opening cupboards and peering in, looking in drawers, even pushing open the door to Olivia's bedroom.

That was a step too far for Queenie. 'Stop that,' she barked.

'You're a feisty one, aren't you?' said the man, giving her a stern look.

'If you don't stop that, you'll see just how feisty I can be,' barked Queenie.

'And me,' barked Duke, baring his teeth.

Lucky for him, Archie arrived, Olivia behind him. 'What's going on? What's making these dogs bark like that? Who are you? And what d'you want?'

The man harrumphed and glared at the dogs. 'Are you Mr Truelove?' he said, 'Mr Archie Truelove, owner of this establishment?'

'I most certainly am,' said Archie. 'And who might you be?'

'I,' said the man self-importantly, 'am the Dog Inspector and I have to inform you, Mr Truelove, that a complaint has been made to the RSPCA about a dangerous dog causing an accident on the place they call The Moors, resulting in a young lady falling from her horse, narrowly escaping serious injury.'

'And…?' said Archie, as Duke sidled under the table.

'And…' said the man, '…we have reason to believe that the guilty party is, in fact, one of your dogs. Having witnessed the behaviour of your dogs for myself, their vicious nature, I am inclined to believe that to be a true assessment of the situation.'

Archie seemed lost for words for a few moments, whilst Olivia, looking frightened, glanced towards Duke hiding under the table.

'It is my job,' continued the man, 'to take custody of such dogs, who prove to be a danger to other people.'

'What?' stuttered Archie.

Olivia went pale and Duke began to tremble as Queenie gave him a nudge.

'Not only that, but a considerable fine is normally levied on the owner of such dogs.'

'You can't do that,' said Archie. 'You can't be sure…'

'I have it on good authority that this young lady,' – he pointed at Olivia – 'was out with a number of dogs yesterday and one of said dogs was the culprit in question.'

'Do you have any proof of that?' demanded Archie.

'We have a very reliable witness, who is

prepared to make a statement to that effect.'

'Witness? What witness?'

'I'm afraid I'm not in a position to reveal the source of my information. I wish to inform you, Mr Truelove, that said offender has been captured and is now in custody.'

Archie and Olivia exchanged puzzled glances and Queenie gave Duke another nudge under the table.

'You have two choices, Mr Truelove. We can either return the dog to you, a black dog with cropped ears and a scarred face, and you can pay the fine, likely to be in the region of one thousand pounds…' Archie and Olivia gasped in unison, '…or we can retain the dog and attempt to find it a suitable home. It's your first offence and so we are prepared to be lenient with you.'

'How do we know you're who you say you are?' said Archie. 'You could be any Tom, Dick or Harry.'

The man pointed to an official-looking badge pinned to his lapel. '**Mr Harold Miller, Dog Inspector for the RSPCA**' was printed in bold black letters, next to his picture. 'Now which is it to be, Mr Truelove? I'm a busy man.'

Archie looked questioningly at Olivia.

'Would you definitely find Blackie a good home?' said Olivia, glancing at Duke, who was gazing pleadingly at her.

'The dog appears to be fairly docile, merely short on training, so we are hopeful, young lady. And you will of course be notified when a new owner has been found for the dog.'

'I think we should do that then, Granddad,' said Olivia. 'At least Blackie will get a good home.'

Queenie felt Duke give a sigh of relief as he stopped shaking and flopped down.

'Very well,' said Archie. 'But we want to know when the dog is rehomed.'

'Absolutely,' said the man, putting his clipboard on the table and producing a pen from his inside pocket. 'I just need you to sign here, and here, granting us custody.' He put his hand over the top page and pointed to the bottom corner and then lifted up the edge and pointed to the bottom corner of the page underneath.

'I'll just get my specs,' said Archie.

'I'm afraid I'm late for my next appointment, Mr Truelove, so if you wouldn't mind just signing and then I'll be on my way. No harm done.' The man held out his pen.

Archie took it from him and scrawled his signature where the man had indicated.

Olivia tried to peer over his shoulder, but the man snatched up the clipboard, did a silly bow, held out his hand and gave Archie a limp handshake. 'Pleasure doing business with you, Mr Truelove. Have a good day. Young lady,' he said, nodding at Olivia. And with that, he was out the door without a backward glance.

***

'Phew, that was a narrow escape,' said Duke once Archie had gone to change the dogs over in the Big Kennels and Olivia was putting Kat back in with her mum and sisters. 'I was really worried for a while there, Queen. I'm going to have to be more careful in future.'

'I don't know, Duke. There was something fishy about all that. It was all too rushed. I think we were all slightly panicked and Archie was obviously worried about the money. I feel uneasy about it. I didn't think that girl was the type to report what happened. Was somebody spying on us on the Moors, I wonder? Or did Laurence tell his dad what happened?'

44. Positive Thinking and Meeting the Fairies

Kat

I'm still only a little pup, getting on for seven weeks old, and my magic powers are still underdeveloped according to Queenie She says they will improve with time and hard work, but that I should concentrate on positive thinking for now. She says it's like believing your food bowl is half full instead of half empty. Whatever. I know Queenie's worried about that man that was here. She didn't like him and I didn't either, but I'm trying not to think about him because that can't be positive thinking. That painting idea of Olivia's sounds as though it could be though, like making the best of things. I'm going to work on that.

Here comes Olivia now to fetch me for my milk and vitamins. I'll see what I can do.

'Hello, little Kat,' she says, picking me up, giving me lots of kisses and blowing into my fur. I like that and I lick her face to show her that she's my most favourite person in the world. She makes a fuss of Mum, who's also very pleased to see her. That's okay, I don't mind that, but then she starts stroking and tickling my sisters. I don't like that much, so I yip a few times and pop my ears up and down. 'All right, Kat,' she says, 'don't be getting jealous now.'

As if!

She tells Mum that she'll come and let her out later and takes me into the place where she sleeps, and I do too sometimes, and puts me on the bed while she starts rummaging in one of her drawers. When she's not looking, I magic myself on to the floor. I don't think Queenie will mind that because I've made sure Olivia doesn't see me doing it and it's a long way for me to jump and I might hurt myself. Then I go over to the box where Olivia keeps her painting set and pick up a small brush in my mouth. I give a muffled yip.

'How did you get off the bed? Did you jump?' says Olivia in a worried voice. 'You could have done yourself an injury, you silly girl. And what's that you've got in your mouth? Is it a paintbrush?'

She picks me up and takes the paintbrush off me. 'What a good idea, Kat,' she says. 'That's what I'll do today, some painting. Now. Where shall we start?'

I've heard Olivia talk about the treehouse and

the faded dragon on the door, which she sounded sad about. Surely making that look nice again is positive thinking. I yip a few times to tell her my idea. 'What's that you're saying, Kat?' she laughs. She looks into my eyes and I concentrate on picturing the treehouse. After a moment, she says, 'D'you know what, Kat? I think I'll start with the door of the treehouse. Yes, that's what I'll do.' One of my ears shoots up in the air and she laughs again. 'Are you agreeing with me, Kat?' I nod my head. 'After you've had your milk, you can go back in with the others whilst I climb up to the treehouse.' *No, no, no*. I shake my head a lot. 'What? You want to come with me?' I nod again. I can tell she's wondering whether it's a good idea or not. Finally she says, 'All right then. I suppose you'll be safe tucked in my T-shirt.' I nod again. Phew. I need to *be* there.

***

I gulp down the milk and vitamins. 'Come on, Olivia,' I yip. She picks up the paintbrush, a bottle of water and her box of paints and puts them in a little bag that she straps to her back. 'We won't tell Granddad until after,' she says. 'We don't want him to worry.'

Once we reach the willow tree, Olivia calls

Oberon, who's eating grass in the far corner of the field. He comes galloping over and nuzzles Olivia's ear. Then he rubs noses with me, which is our way of saying hello. I like Oberon, even though Queenie doesn't say very nice things about him. Olivia puts me in the bag on her back. She calls it a rucksack. My head peeps out the top, so I can see everything.

'Can you help us up, please, Oberon,' says Olivia and Oberon kneels down on his front legs. Olivia climbs on to Oberon's back. She wobbles a little when he stands up and then grasps hold of one of the branches and steps on to another. 'Thanks, Oberon,' she says and he neighs and gallops off.

Olivia climbs carefully up the tree, branch by branch, chattering away to me. It's all terribly exciting. I really like this positive thinking thing. When we reach the treehouse, Olivia settles astride one of the branches as if she's riding Oberon and takes off her bag. 'I think we'll go purple again,' she says, stroking the faint outline of the little dragon on the door.

'Yes, yes,' I yip, as she puts me on her knee. That makes her laugh for some reason.

She dips her brush into the bottle of water and then into the block of purple paint, swishes it about and starts with the outline of the dragon.

I can tell she's really concentrating as her tongue keeps popping out of the side of her mouth. She paints on some scales in black and gives the dragon a really kind eye and a pointy tail. I always thought dragons were wicked, but she's made this one look really sweet. Rather like me.

'Shall we add a little flame coming out of its mouth?' she says.

'Yes, yes,' I yip again.

'Whatever you say, Kat.' She mixes a little red and yellow paint together and, in no time, the dragon looks like it's breathing fire.

As she puts down her brush, the dragon starts to come alive. It glows and it flashes and looks like it might actually take flight any minute.

'Blimey. What's happening?' says Olivia.

'That's fantastic,' I bark at her. 'You're so clever, Olivia.'

The flashing abruptly stops and the dragon becomes just a painting again.

'I wonder…' says Olivia, reaching forward and tapping on the door three times.

The door flies open and suddenly the air is filled with a blur of little wings and the whisper of tiny voices. 'Here we are, Olivia and Kat,' they sing, fluttering around our heads and dancing in Olivia's hair. 'Welcome back. We're so happy to see you. Thank you. Thank you.'

Olivia's mouth falls open and she looks, I really don't like to say this about my Olivia, but she looks actually quite stupid. Her mouth moves up and down like the fish in the pond, but no words come out.

One of the floaty beings, slightly larger than the others, with beautiful, delicate wings, hovers in front of us, like a bee, only much prettier. 'I am Belle de Jour, also known as Aurora, Queen of the Fairies,' she says, with a little bow, 'so pleased to meet you finally, dear Olivia.'

She's gorgeous with a face almost as lovely as Olivia's. She has long, dark curls and is wearing a shimmery, silvery dress. Gold sparks are shooting out of a tiny wand she's holding in one of her hands.

'Oh,' says Olivia finally. 'I've never seen anything more exquisite in all my life.'

'Thank you, dear Olivia. And thank you for setting us free.'

'Setting you free?'

'We have been locked up for many years, nobody caring for us. You have brought us back to life. I see you're wearing your dear mother's amulet. I gifted it to her many years ago because *she* cared for us. Did you know the amulet has magic powers? If you should ever be in desperate need, the amulet will help you. Clasp it to your heart and make a wish. But use it wisely for it can grant only three wishes and each wish lasts only as long as it takes to complete what you need to do. Then you will have no memory of it. Remember this, dear friend, you and Kat here,' – she nods in my direction – 'can accomplish great things together.'

'That's a bit tight, sis. Three wishes? Give the girl seven. She's probably going to need them.' Behind Aurora, another fairy is flitting back and forth, waving her wand about like she's conducting a piece of music.

'Wow! Are you a goth?' says Olivia.

I'm not sure what a goth is, but I think it might be something to do with the fairy's appearance. She's wearing a black net dress, which sparkles in the sunlight filtering through the branches, and she has a black headdress of little antlers, like a deer's, perched on the snow-white hair, which curls prettily around her face. Her eyes, which have heavy black lines around them, twinkle mischievously. I like her. She winks at us. 'A sort of goth, if you like. My sister doesn't approve. But who cares? Not me. She likes to think she's the boss, but I wield as much, if not more, power than her. Isn't that right, sis, dear? And then, of course, I'm also the good-looking one.'

Aurora, looking sulky, turns her back on her

sister.

'Belle de Nuit, otherwise known as Crepuscola, the other Queen of the Fairies, at your service.' Crepuscola bows, sweeping down her glittering silver wand. 'You stick with me, kids, and you won't go far wrong. Goody Two Shoes here – she nods in Aurora's direction – likes to toe the line. But where's the fun in that? Cheers for letting us out by the way. I was getting very bored with just this one and our minions for company.'

Angry sparks fly out of Aurora's wand. 'She'll lead you astray, Olivia. Just remember that. I'm the one you can rely on.'

'And I'm the one that'll let you have seven wishes, Olivia.'

'It's against the rules,' says Aurora sharply, turning towards her sister. 'You'll get us and them into all kinds of trouble.'

'What did I tell you? Rules, rules, rules. Boring, boring, boring. See you, kids. Don't forget, I'm the fun fairy. Cheers.' Crepuscola waves her magic wand and vanishes.

Olivia seems to have been struck dumb. That daft expression has come back on her face and her mouth's hanging open again. It's not an attractive look.

'I must be going too, dear friends. Call on me when you're in need,' says Aurora, waving her wand and vanishing along with all her little followers.

'Aurora, Crepuscola, where have you gone? Please come back,' shouts Olivia, suddenly coming to life. 'There's so much I need to ask you.'

It's too late. It's only the two of us again. Olivia looks at me and I look at her.

'Did that really happen, Kat?' she says. 'Did we just meet two Fairy Queens? Or am I dreaming?'

My ears are popping up and down of their own accord. 'It happened, Olivia,' I yip. 'We can do anything together. Aurora said so. And Crepuscola is going to give us lots of wishes.'

Olivia nods as if she's understood what I've been saying. Then she packs up her bag, puts me in it, and straps it to her back. 'Come on, let's go and tell Granddad. I'm not sure he'll believe me though. I'm not sure I believe it myself.'

I can't wait to tell Queenie and Duke. This is the best thing that's ever happened to me. I'm really loving this positive thinking and meeting two amazing Fairy Queens. I can't decide which one I like better.

45. A Man with a Briefcase

Shall I tell Granddad about the treehouse, Mum? You've met Aurora, because she gave you the amulet, and probably Crepuscola too. I wish I knew what to do. Can't you help me?

Olivia sighed. It seemed unlikely that Granddad would believe her. She could hardly blame him. It sounded far-fetched even to her. Fairy Queens? Three wishes? Seven wishes? He'd think she was deranged. Did she fall asleep and imagine it? She wound a lock of hair round her forefinger as she sat at the table in the garden nursing Kat and pondering where to go from here.

'Penny for them, love,' said Archie, making her jump as he came up behind her.

Before she could reply, a man with a briefcase came round the corner. It was the same sleazeball in a poncy suit that had been down before, saying he wanted to buy one of the pups. Kat went stiff in her arms, her coat sticking up on end, ears flat to her head.

'Ah, Mr Truelove,' he said holding out his hand.

'Do I know you?' said Granddad, hesitating before he shook the man's hand. 'You look familiar.'

'Er, yes, we have met once before, I believe.'

'I know you. You're that flaming fracking fella, aren't you?'

'It's him again, Granddad, the one who knew my name.'

'Is it now?'

Olivia stared at the man. This felt all wrong.

Queenie, who was at Archie's feet, began growling.

Duke appeared at the kitchen door and began barking.

'Quiet, Duke,' said Granddad and then turned back to the man. 'What d'you want? I told you before, I'm not interested in anything you've got to say.'

The man cleared his throat and gave his briefcase a shake.

'I'm acting as agent for the buyer, Mr Truelove.'

'Buyer? What buyer?' Granddad's voice was getting louder by the second.

'The buyer for your property,' said the man. 'The buyer wishes to know when you will be in a position to vacate the premises.'

'How many times do I have to tell you people?' Granddad was practically shouting by now and going bright red in the face. 'I'm not selling. Not now. Not anytime. Now clear off before I set the dogs on you.'

'I strongly advise against that, Mr Truelove,' said the man, going a similar colour to Granddad. 'I think you'll find I have every right to be here.' He opened his briefcase and took out a sheaf of papers, placing them on the table. 'Here's a copy of the agreement you signed.'

'What?' said Archie. 'I've not signed no agreement.'

'This is your signature, is it not?' said the man, pointing to the bottom of one of the papers.

'What are you talking about, man?' said Archie. 'I've signed nowt.' He snatched up the papers and peered at them. 'I can't see a thing without me specs,' he muttered. 'Have a look what it says, Olivia.'

Archie passed Olivia the papers and she began reading through them, placing a reassuring hand on Kat, who was beginning to tremble. 'Oh,' she gasped.

'What is it?' said Granddad impatiently.

'It says here, Granddad, that you've agreed to sell Kymera at a price to be agreed by Mr Truelove Junior.'

'What? What nonsense is this?' yelled Archie, snatching the papers back.

'I think it's that thing you signed about Blackie,' said Olivia. 'You remember that man was in a rush and you just signed it.'

'That's ridiculous. I didn't even read it properly. This can't be legal.'

'I'm afraid it's very much legal,' said the man, looking far too smug for Olivia's liking. 'Are you in the habit of signing papers without reading them first, Mr Truelove?'

'The chap was in a hurry,' blustered Archie, squinting at the papers again, 'and so was I. Some of us have proper work to do, you know. This is a swindle pure and simple and this is what I think of your swindle.' Archie held the papers in his two hands, tore them in half and screwed them up. 'There. Now, what d'you have to say?'

The man snapped his briefcase shut and placed it near his feet. 'I'm afraid that won't do any good at all, Mr Truelove. These papers are merely copies. The originals are in a safe place. It would be in your interests…'

'I tell you what would be in *your* interests, Mr Swindler,' said Archie, who was beginning to resemble a turkey cock with his purple face and bulging eyes, 'and that is to get off my property before I throw you off. If I ever set eyes on you again, you'll be hearing from my solicitor.'

Olivia had never seen Archie so angry. He

was practically spitting at the man. Her heart was beating so violently, she thought it was about to burst out of her chest. Kat gave her an anxious look and then looked over to Duke, who was standing at the kitchen door. She seemed to nod in the direction of the man's briefcase and, next thing, Duke came bounding down the steps, seized the briefcase in his mouth and made off with it.

'What the…?' said the man, puffing his cheeks out and looking like a bewildered hamster. 'Get my briefcase off that dog right now.'

'Get it yourself,' said Archie.

The man scowled and scurried off after Duke, who was heading for the back field. 'Come back here, you little villain,' he yelled.

Olivia looked at Granddad and Granddad looked at Olivia and they both stood up and followed the man. They watched him chase Duke across the back field, breaking into a run as Duke stopped and appeared to be waiting for him to catch up. When the man was nearly upon him, Duke slipped under the barbed wire fence, the briefcase still in his mouth, and headed off down the lane towards the Moors.

The man stumbled and fell, getting himself all tangled up in the barbed wire. 'Don't just stand there, come and help me,' he shouted at Olivia and Archie, who looked at each other.

'What d'you think, Olivia?' said Granddad.

'I think you'd better go and see to the dogs in the Big Kennels, Granddad.'

'And I think you'd better go and get that kettle on,' said Archie. 'I can feel a thirst coming on.'

'And what do *you* think, Kat?' said Olivia, looking down at her.

'Yip, yip,' went Kat, one ear shooting up in the air.

'What about you, Queenie?' said Archie.

'Yap, yap, yap,' went Queenie.

'Have you even got a solicitor, Granddad?' said Olivia.

'No that I know of,' said Archie. 'Where d'you get them from?'

Putting his arm round her, Archie winked and the two of them turned their back on the man and set off laughing as they headed back to Ky Manor.

The dogs sounded like they were joining in as they barked and pranced around as if they were at a party.

46. Fat Cat Pink Dog

'What d'you mean he's gone away? Gone where?'

Queenie gazed anxiously at Archie as he shouted down the phone to Janey, Nick's wife. 'Well, tell him to phone me the minute he gets back. Or better still, tell him to get down here. I want to know what the heck he thinks he's playing at.' Archie slammed the phone down, scowled and headed for the bathroom. Queenie could hear him 'swilling his face off', which she knew meant he was pretty riled up.

Queenie glanced over at Duke, who was looking rather pleased with himself, having dumped the briefcase in the dyke and slipped back to Kymera unseen.

Olivia came into the kitchen, with Kat in her arms and Katja frolicking round her feet like a little puppy.

'I think it's time you had a little coaching in magic, Kat,' said Queenie. 'Nothing too fancy, but I've a feeling that we're not going to get out of this mess without *some* magic.'

'Look out, Queenie's got a "feeling",' said Duke.

Queenie gave him a disparaging look as Kat

began to struggle in Olivia's arms.

'You want to go down, do you?' said Olivia. 'All right, down you go. Have a little play. I'm going to get changed.'

Olivia disappeared into her bedroom and Kat scampered over to her mum, who was conversing with Queenie and Duke. 'Magic?' she said breathily. 'I thought magic wasn't allowed.'

'Normally not,' said Queenie, 'but these are exceptional circumstances. Kymera is in danger. There are some devilish dealings afoot. Come on, let's go outside, out of the way of the humans. But don't draw attention to yourselves.'

Queenie, Duke, Kat and Katja headed stealthily towards the kitchen door as Olivia emerged from her bedroom. 'And where do you lot think you're going?'

Kat gazed pleadingly at Olivia, who laughed. 'All right then, but make sure you all look after Kat. Queenie, Duke, Katja, think on. Remember she's only a little pup. Don't be getting up to any mischief. And don't go far.'

All the dogs nodded as Kat jumped up and down excitedly on the spot. 'Yes, magic,' she barked. 'Magic, magic.'

Fortunately Olivia didn't understand what she was saying and just smiled indulgently as she sat down to scroll through her phone.

'Right, I think we need to start with keywords. The secret to a good spell is the mantra.'

Kat looked blankly at Queenie. 'The what?'

'When I'm casting spells,' said Queenie importantly, 'I have a little ditty, you know, a rhyme for each occasion. Never fails. Unless I get it wrong. You should do the same or things can get all out of control. You need to find what works for you. It's like word association…'

'Blah, blah, blah. Get on with it, Queenie, old girl…'

'I think we'll start with Teleportation,' said Queenie, ignoring Duke's crass remark.

'Actually, I'd better get back to my pups,' said Katja. 'They'll want feeding. D'you want to help yourself, Kat, before I go?'

Katja lay on her side and Kat rushed over and started sucking greedily on one of her teats.

'For DogGod's sake,' said Queenie after a few moments, 'can we please just get on with this magic lesson? There's time for food later. Remember what's at stake.'

At the mention of magic, Kat stopped suckling and scampered back over to Queenie.

Meanwhile, Duke had decided there were some interesting smells in the vicinity of a group of young saplings Archie had planted and was snuffling about and cocking his leg where the fancy took him.

'So,' said Queenie, 'teleportation. You've already shown some ability with that. You just need to be able to control it better. Let's start with a keyword, one you'll associate with teleporting yourself.'

'Telly what?' said Kat. 'Never heard of it.'

'It means getting from one place to another without using your legs, nitwit,' said Duke, who'd wandered back over. 'Like when you got up the Manor steps without climbing them and Queenie nearly had you roasted for dinner for showing off.'

'Ha, ha, Duke.' Kat bounced up and down on the spot. 'Yes, I get it. It's a bit like that thing birds do – flying. I don't think I really need one of those keyword whatsits, although I quite like the sound of "whizz". How about this?

'Ruler over sky and sea,

'Whizz me where I need to be.

'I like it.' Kat wagged her tail, looking a touch smug.

'It's got a certain ring to it,' admitted Queenie. 'Very well, give it a go. Try teleporting yourself to the willow tree. Focus and chant. Focus and chant.'

Kat shut her eyes tight, repeating her little phrase, and immediately vanished. A short while later, she reappeared, one ear flopped down, the other stuck straight up in the air.

'Sorry about that,' she said. 'Just as I shut my eyes, the thought of Mum and milk popped into my head and there I was, back amongst my boring old sisters, fighting for Mum's attention.'

'*FCPD: Fat Cat Pink Dog*. Absolutely essential in magic,' snapped Queenie.

'What the heck's that, Queen?' said Duke. 'It sounds right daft.'

'It stands for *Focus, Control, Practice, Discipline*, Duke. Something you'd know nothing about. They're the four precepts, the four cornerstones, of magical practice.'

'Get *you*, Boss Bitch. "Precepts" indeed. I think she's getting a bit too posh for us, eh, Kat?'

Kat was looking baffled. And that's putting it politely.

'I know you're only just starting out, Kat,' said Queenie kindly, 'but there can be no room for error. You must focus at all times or things could go drastically wrong. Try again. With focus this time.'

'That means you need to concentrate, Kat Rat,' said Duke. 'In case you were wondering.'

Kat closed her eyes and chanted. Poof. She was gone. Disappeared. Moments later she reappeared at the foot of the willow tree, looking rather too pleased with herself for Queenie's liking.

'Right. Now again.'

'Again? How many times?'

'As many times as I say, young lady. Practice makes perfect. How d'you think I got where I am today? Through hard work, that's how. Again, I say.

'Now to the stable…

'Now the other end of the field…

And so it went on, until there was a sudden loud clap of thunder and menacing, dark clouds scooted across the previously clear sky.

Queenie glanced round in time to see a white figure skedaddling in the direction of the Big Kennels.

'That wretched Pookah dog again,' said Queenie. 'I'm sure she's somehow managing to channel Malina.'

'Here we go,' said Duke. 'It couldn't just be a normal change in the weather, could it? It does happen, you know, Queen. Not every small black cloud means Malina's on the warpath and wanting to get her gnashers round young Kat here.'

'I want my mum,' whispered Kat, crouching down and flattening her ears. 'I don't like this.'

47. Archie is Cross and Olivia is Upset

KAT

I'm not going to lie, I'm frightened. I wish Queenie wouldn't talk about this Malina. She sounds ever so scary. Duke seems to think she only exists in Queenie's mind. I hope he's right. Only Olivia really makes me feel safe. She'll not let anything happen to me, I'm sure.

The weather seems to have gone right again and me and Olivia are sitting in the garden with Archie, who's not looking very happy. His eyebrows are all scrunched up like he's thinking very hard and it's hurting. I should imagine thinking very hard *does* hurt. I wouldn't like to do it. Olivia's playing with my ears and Queenie and Duke are having a minor squabble under the table when Laurence and Felix come around the corner. Olivia nudges Archie, who stands up and shouts, 'Is your dad with you? Where's your dad?'

'And good afternoon to you too, Granddad,' says Laurence in a jolly voice. Queenie thinks he's very handsome for a human and I can see what she means. His black hair looks much silker even than mine.

They both come and shake Archie's hand, a strange habit humans seem to enjoy doing, although Archie doesn't seem so sure about it today. They give Olivia a peck on the cheek. Laurence touches her hair and tells her she looks nice. She goes all red. I know she doesn't like it when that happens, but she can't seem to help it when Laurence is around.

'Dad's gone away for a couple of days with Grandma Sylvia,' says Felix. 'I'm not sure where.'

That seems to make Archie mad. 'No wonder your mother didn't want to tell me where he'd gone,' he shouts. 'It wouldn't surprise me if *she,* bloomin' Sylvia, I mean, was behind all this trickery to try and sell this place from under me.' His voice is starting to hurt my ears.

Felix and Laurence glance at each other and then away again.

'What do you two know about it? Eh? Are you in on it too?'

'Granddad!' says Olivia in a shocked voice.

'In on what, Gramps?'

'Don't play the innocent with me. I'm surprised at you, Felix. At both of you. You know how much the place means to me and Olivia.'

Archie has gone even redder than Olivia, and wisps of grey hair are sticking out of the sides of his cap, quivering like little wings. 'I'm going to change the dogs,' he shouts, leaping up in a very unArchie-like way. 'Make them a cup of tea, Olivia, and then we'll have a serious talk when I get back.'

***

Archie stomps off and Olivia hands me over to Felix. 'Here,' she says, 'hold Kat for a minute, while I go and put the kettle on.'

'No sugar in mine, thanks, Liv,' says Laurence.

'Nor me,' says Felix. 'I'm trying to lose a bit of weight.'

I can't argue with that, but his tummy's very soft and comfy, I have to say.

Once Olivia has disappeared into the kitchen, Laurence leans in towards Felix. 'What are we going to say to Granddad? He's really upset.'

'I know, but what can we do? Dad reckons the place has to go. I don't know what's going on with him and Grandma Sylvia. She seems to be calling the shots. We've spent a lot of our childhood here, Laurence. I'd much rather we kept Kymera in the family.'

'There's something Dad's not telling us.'

Laurence leans in even further towards Felix and whispers in his ear. 'I heard him talking with Grandma Syl. He said something about getting you "out of this mess".'

I gaze up at Felix, who looks shocked. 'Me? Out of what mess? I don't know what you're talking about.'

'Something about it "being in the blood",' says Laurence, pushing a lock of hair behind his ear, which somehow makes him look even more handsome. 'I was listening outside the door. I didn't know whether to say anything to you.'

'"In the blood?" What the heck's that supposed to mean?'

Yes, what is that supposed to mean? I don't like this talk of blood.

'And she told Dad that he needed to get his hands on this little pup here.'

'What? Kat?' says Felix, looking down at me. 'What do they want with Kat? That's weird.'

I feel a flash of fear, but try not to tremble. Nobody must know I can understand human speech. Otherwise Queenie will be very cross. I know she's listening to everything they're saying from under the table. I try and look stupid by imitating the cross-eyed face that Duke sometimes puts on when he's joking about with Queenie.

I don't imagine they're finding *this* conversation very funny.

'I don't really know what's going on,' says Laurence, looking at me as if I've suddenly grown an extra head, 'but we need to decide on a strategy. We should have worked out what to say before we came down. Watch out now. Olivia's coming back. Just follow my lead.'

Olivia puts a tray with a teapot, milk and cups on the table. She's not looking her usual smiley self. Normally she's practically swooning when Laurence is around. That's what Queenie says anyhow.

'Did your dad send that man down? The one who tricked Granddad into signing something he shouldn't,' says Olivia as she pours milk into the cups, not looking at either of them.

'I don't know anything about that, Liv.' Laurence takes the milk bottle off her and grasps her hand, pulling her down on to the seat next to him. 'Listen, I think Dad's got money troubles…'

'Well, that's not our fault,' says Olivia.

'I know it isn't, sweetheart, but he might be forced to sell little Kat, and you wouldn't want that, would you?'

Olivia blushes and snatches her hand back. She looks all hot and bothered as she grabs me roughly off Felix. 'He'll not be selling *my* dog,' she yells at Laurence. 'Granddad will never let him do that.

'And I'm not your sweetheart,' she adds after a moment, looking down at the ground.

'Come on, Liv, don't be like that,' says Laurence in a gentle voice and giving Olivia's arm a stroke. 'I'm sure Dad wants you to keep Kat, but I think the money situation might be serious. And he really does think it's time Granddad retired, and that you'd both be better off in a proper house with some money.'

'Well, you can tell him that he's wrong,' says Olivia in a shaky voice, water filling her eyes. 'We won't be better off in a "proper house", because we won't be moving. And he won't be selling Kat either. He can jolly well find the money somewhere else.'

'He only wants what's best for everyone. Isn't that right, Felix?' says Laurence, staring hard at him.

Felix nods but he looks all glum and his eyes look all watery, like Olivia's.

I snuggle up close to her. I don't like this. Why can't everybody just be nice?

Archie slams the gate to the Big Kennels shut and comes stomping towards us. He goes to sit down at the table, but then jumps up again. 'I'm not going to discuss it with you two boys,' he says, 'coming to Kymera and upsetting my granddaughter like this.' Olivia and I both look up at him. *My granddaughter*? 'You can tell your father that I can't be softened up by a couple of jackasses. He needs to get himself down here. Now I'd like you to leave me and my granddaughter in peace.'

'What about our tea, Granddad?' says Laurence. 'You'll be sending us to bed without any supper next.'

'Never mind all that,' says Archie. 'This is no laughing matter.'

That's something I can agree with. *I* certainly wouldn't like to be sent to bed without any supper, which I think is another word for food.

Laurence and Felix look at each other and pull a funny face as they stand up.

Felix holds out his hand. 'Please don't let's fall out, Gramps. We all love Kymera. Just like you do.'

Archie folds his arms and turns and looks the other way. Queenie always says he can be as stubborn as a mule when he wants to be. I think this is what she means.

I feel a bit sorry for Laurence and Felix as they wander off down the path without another word. But then I look at my Olivia's face and the only person I feel sorry for is her.

48. Queenie is Discombobulated

Queenie

'Well, well, well,' said Queenie. 'I don't know.'

'What don't you know, oh Wise One?'

'Shut up, Duke. 'I'm thinking.'

Queenie had only ever heard Archie call Olivia 'my granddaughter' when he was introducing her to somebody he didn't know very well, and that time when he rang up the local school to see if they could take her. Never in front of Laurence and Felix. And what was sly Sylvia doing sniffing around? Sylvia was the Malina of the human world in Queenie's eyes. Why was she so interested in Kat? What did she want her for? And there was the stuff about 'blood' too. That couldn't be good. Queenie shuddered. Everything felt wrong.

'What d'you reckon to that blood business, Duke?' she said.

'I don't reckon owt,' said Duke, scratching his ear under the garden table. 'That's humans for you, isn't it? They're a breed apart. Who knows what's going on in their heads? I didn't like what Laurence said about selling Kat though. I've got kind of used to the little rat being around. Not that I'm saying that I'd miss her exactly. Hey, *I've* got an idea. Why doesn't she turn Old Nick into a toad?'

'This is a no joking matter, Duke,' snapped Queenie. 'All our lives are at stake here. We need a plan.'

'Keep your coat on, old girl,' said Duke. 'We'll figure something out, don't you fret. You can always rely on your second-in-command.'

'Let's call a meeting,' said Queenie.

'And who exactly are we inviting to this meeting, Queen?'

'Kat, Valentino…'

'Queenie Two, Old Soldier? I'm sure they'll all have important contributions to make,' said Duke, nodding.

He had a point. Valentino could follow simple orders, but Queenie Two's main interest, in fact only interest in life, was food. And Soldier would be willing, but not actually able. Kat might shape up though. 'Go and find Kat, Duke, and tell her to come to Archie's bedroom.'

***

Duke appeared at the bedroom door, with Kat in his mouth. He dropped her on the floor in a fluffy heap. 'She said she wanted to stay near Olivia, even though I told her she'd been summoned, Queen. Such insubordination. I don't know, youngsters today.' Duke shook his head.

'I'm worried about Olivia,' whined Kat. 'She's very sad.'

'Never mind that,' said Duke. 'How d'you fancy turning Old Nick into a toad? That's the question.'

'A toad? Really?' said Kat, flicking up one of her ears. 'I think I can manage that.'

'Ignore him, Kat,' said Queenie impatiently. 'We need to save Kymera and we need to stop Sylvia getting her hands on you. She's capable of anything, that woman. She's the human version of Malina.'

Kat's smug expression changed to one of sheer terror as Duke did a little cough, obviously an attempt to hide a snigger. One day that lad would realize just how dangerous Malina and Sylvia could be. At his peril, if he wasn't careful.

'Firstly, we need to get our paws on those papers,' said Queenie. 'Don't be worrying, Kat, Archie will never agree to you being sold. And he'll certainly not let Sylvia near you. I think he hates that woman nearly as much as I do. But then again, he has let her worm her way into his life twice. Humans have this funny habit of pretending not to like someone when really they do, especially when it's a man and a woman. It's strange. They're not like us dogs that way.'

'Oh, I don't know, Queenie, old girl. There have been times when I've thought you didn't like *me*, when I know you actually think I'm a handsome fella and probably wouldn't say no if I were bold enough to ask.'

'Don't be ridiculous, Duke,' said Queenie with a snarl. 'Of course I like you most of the time, but you can also be very irritating. As for anything else…in your dreams, soft lad.'

***

Unable to come up with a definite plan, Queenie decided that, if the situation really called for it, then Kat should be allowed to use a little magic, provided she was discreet, and Queenie herself might even do the same. She would instruct Valentino to listen out for any orders and obey them instantly and Duke would make sure nobody came to any harm. They would need to keep a close eye on Pookah as she may be part of the plot to steal Kat and sell Kymera. Queenie felt quite discombobulated, a word Archie liked to use when he was out of sorts. It always made Olivia laugh. *Discombobulated, Granddad? Are you sure you haven't just made that up?*

Queenie was wondering whether to have a snooze to revitalize her brain cells or go and check on Archie. She never liked to have him out of her sight for too long, especially when he was no doubt feeling as discombobulated as *she* was. A sudden commotion outside made the decision for her. She hurtled out to find Archie shouting all sorts of things he really shouldn't at yet another man waving around a bunch of papers. A couple of men were standing behind him and, behind them, she saw Old Nick, looking worried and sheepish at the same time, Pookah at his heels. Valentino was barking loudly and Olivia was clutching Kat and crying. Duke was nowhere to be seen.

49. Kat Steps Up

Kat

I hate to see my Olivia crying. Here's Queenie now, looking very cross. Maybe *she'll* know what to do. Archie's rattling a bucket and shouting, Get off my land and take your stupid papers with you! His face is red like a tomato and he's shaking his fist.

The man waving papers is saying, It's all legal and above board, Mr Truelove. You've sold the place to me and my colleagues. I've a cheque here for both you and your son. The sale has been agreed. Come along now. Be reasonable.

Reasonable? yells Archie. I'll show you 'reasonable'. He looks like he might explode any second and Queenie looks at him anxiously as he strides over towards the man, a murderous expression on his face. He gives the man a shove and then marches over to Old Nick and pokes him in the chest several times. You traitor, you ne'er do well, he shouts. You're no son of mine.

I don't know what a ne'er do well is, but I don't think it's a good thing.

It's for the best, Dad, for you and Olivia, stutters Nasty Nick.

Olivia's shouting, Stop it, all of you. Just stop it. I can feel her shaking.

Suddenly Queenie shoots over and nips the man with the papers on the ankle. He starts hopping and shouting some rude words, words which Queenie has told me I must never use and I've only heard Archie say once or twice. Then Pookah rushes over and attacks Queenie. They're barking really loud and biting each other. Pookah has grabbed Queenie round the throat.

Olivia starts screaming and I'm struggling in her arms, not knowing what to do. Where's Duke when you need him?

Valentino rushes over and throws himself into the middle of the fighting. Go, Dad!

All I can see is fur flying, snapping teeth and a muddle of bodies.

Then Old Soldier totters over and stands barking his funny bark, which he does because he's deaf, or so Queenie says. Good old Granddad.

Even Queenie Two comes out of the kitchen, a biscuit in her mouth, drops it and races over barking angrily like I've never heard her bark before. She bares her teeth and throws herself into the middle of the fight. Nice one, Gran!

Archie drops the bucket he's still carrying,

runs over and aims a kick in amongst the fighting dogs, but they carry on. I think one of them has bitten his foot as he starts hopping like the man was doing before and saying rude words.

I need to do something, but I seem unable to move and Olivia is gripping me very tightly.

Archie picks up the bucket and scoops up some water from the pond. He throws it at the fighting dogs and they stop for a moment and then carry on.

I start shaking along with Olivia.

Suddenly Duke appears. He must have been visiting Oberon. He looks at me and barks, Do something, Kat. Quick.

I'm still frozen and useless.

Archie fills up the bucket again, but he slips and crashes to the ground, water spilling everywhere. More bad words come out of Archie's mouth. Duke leaps over him and is about to launch himself into the middle of the fighting dogs, when Olivia squeezes me even tighter and grasps her mum's necklace with her spare hand, shuts her eyes and says, Please make all this stop. Please, please, please.

A strange feeling comes over me. There's nothing I can't do. Put me down, Olivia, I say. She places me on the ground without speaking. Her eyes have gone funny like she can't see properly.

Duke pauses and glances round at me.

'*Stop this fight now,*

'I care not how,' I chant in my head.

A beam of light shoots from my eyes and lands in the middle of the fighting dogs. They pull apart and stand staring at each other. Queenie's legs seem to go from under her. Duke starts licking her where she's bleeding and Queenie Two joins in. Valentino and Pookah continue to glare at one another.

Archie gets up off the ground and brushes himself down.

I turn to look at the man who was waving the papers about before. He's standing with his mouth open, looking rather stupid.

'*Let flame and fire,*

'Consume this liar.'

As the words form like magic in my head, the light shoots out of my eyes again and the papers in the man's hand burst into flames. He drops them with a scream and then starts stamping on them, trying to put the fire out. The two men behind him rush forward and bend down to pick up the burning papers but yell out in pain and pull their hands back. The papers carry on burning until there's nothing left but ash.

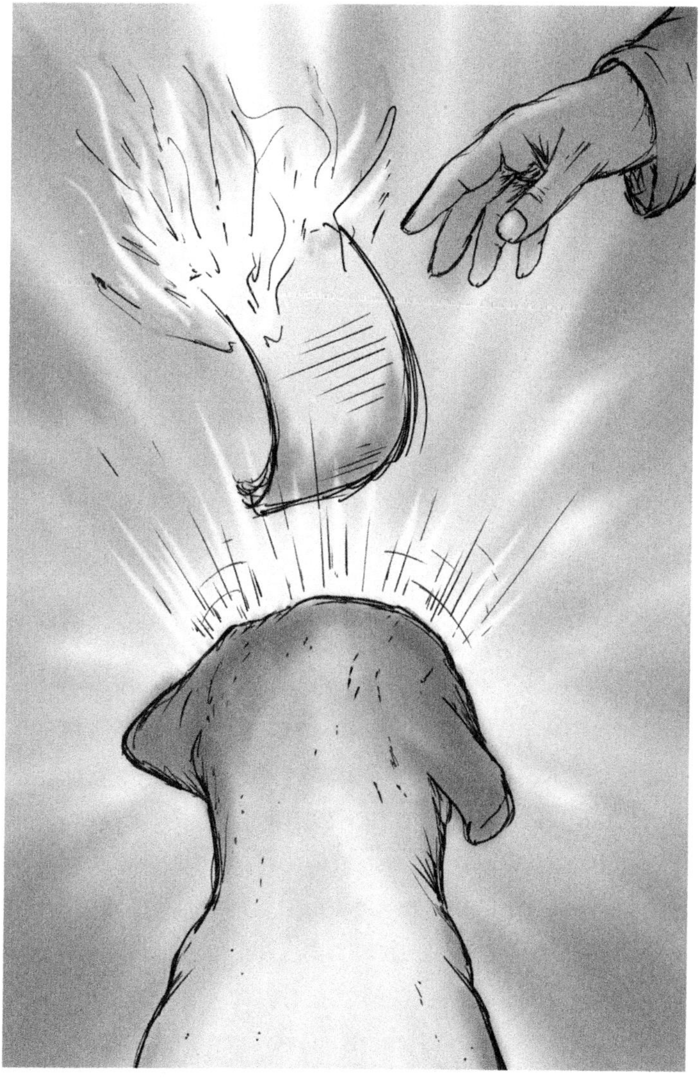

Old Nick has gone very white and points a shaky finger at me. Contaminated, he whispers. That dog is contaminated.

You know nothing, Old Nick. You have no idea what I'm capable of and, for your sake, I hope you never have to find out. Although I might actually enjoy turning you into a big, fat, ugly toad.

***

'Right, clear off, you lot.' Archie's voice booms very loud. He's waving his hands around. 'You heard what I said. Now, get off my land right now and don't show your faces here again or you'll get what's coming to you.'

The men look at each other and then towards Nick, who gives them a brief nod. They slink off like foxes in the night, the one who had the papers limping and muttering under his breath. Nick makes to follow them.

'That's right. You get gone 'n all and take that mutt with you.' Archie points to Pookah, who's shivering, tail down, at Nick's feet. 'I don't want to see either of you down here again.'

'But Dad…'

Archie waves a dismissive hand at him. 'You heard what I said, lad. Now get gone. I've these dogs to see to. My Queenie'd better be all right after this, or there'll be hell to pay. You mark my words.'

50. Olivia Has a Plan

'You did well there, Kat. I'm proud of you.' Queenie was lying in a fluffy bed in the kitchen, licking her wounds. Archie had fussed over her, bathed her with great care and then dragged out the soft, fluffy bed from under his bed, where he'd put it when Queenie had taken to sleeping with him. In *his* bed.

'Come on, old girl,' he'd said gruffly, placing her gently in it. 'You rest now. You're a grand little dog, a real heroine.'

It was nice to be called that even if Queenie knew that Kat was the real heroine of the day.

Valentino and Queenie Two only had a few minor scratches, but were still resting up in the front room. Valentino had gone above and beyond and surprised everyone. Queenie Two had done well too, but then she loved nothing better than a good scrap, apart from a good meal of course.

Duke was hovering around anxiously. He cleared his throat as he glanced at Queenie. 'You may be a pain in the rump at times, Queen, but I wouldn't like to be without you.'

'Don't you be getting all soppy on me, Duke,'

said Queenie, preening. 'This is no time for sentimentality. We may have seen off the enemy for now, but they could be regrouping for a second attack.'

'But those papers have gone,' said Kat, fluffing out her coat. 'I made them disappear.'

'There are bound to be copies,' said Queenie. 'There always are.'

Kat pushed out her bottom lip like a sulky pup and pressed her ears close to her head. 'You mean I haven't saved Kymera after all?'

'You did us proud, Kat,' said Queenie. 'It's given everyone something to think about and, crucially, we now have time to plan our next move. And you were very discreet. You're shaping up to be a Lupina we can all look up to.'

Kat's ears shot up and down at this remark.

'Or down to, eh, pipsqueak?' said Duke, towering over her.

Kat's little face crumpled.

'Take no notice of the old codger,' said Queenie. 'He's just jealous because he was messing about with that daft horse he seems so fond of, instead of being at the scene and doing his job properly.'

'Pffft,' said Duke. 'Even *I* can't be all places at all times. I…'

He was interrupted by a loud *YES!* that came

from the sitting room, where Olivia had been messing about on her laptop.

She came bounding into the kitchen. 'Hey, dogs,' she said excitedly. 'I've been googling some things…' The dogs all looked blankly at each other. '…and, apparently, it's not legal what Uncle Nick and those nasty men have done. You can't just trick somebody into signing away their home. You can be done for that.'

'Done for what?' said Archie, coming into the kitchen and putting the kettle on the stove, after giving it a shake to see how much water there was in it.

'Do you *know* any solicitors, Granddad? We can fight Uncle Nick and those men who are after Kymera legally. They can't trick you into signing the place away, just like that.'

Archie turned round to look at her. 'And where am I supposed to find money for solicitors, Olivia?' He shook his head. 'No, but I tell you something. We won't be moving either. We'll just stay put. They'll have to carry me out of here feet first.'

Queenie barked her approval and the other dogs joined in as back-up.

Olivia sat down at the table and patted the seat next to her. 'Come and sit down, Granddad. I've got a plan.'

Archie made some tea, poured a bowlful out for Queenie, adding some cold water, so that she wouldn't burn her mouth, and put it down next to her. He patted her on the head. 'There you go, Queenie. You're a very brave dog, the best I've ever had, but you're getting a bit old for scrapping and I want you around for as long as possible.'

Queenie was surprised to see a tear slide down Archie's face, the big softie. He wiped it away quickly before Olivia noticed. Poor Archie. All this stress was really getting to him and it made Queenie's heart hurt. Nobody, but nobody, was allowed to mess with her Archie and upset him like that.

Archie put the teapot on the table with a couple of cups and a milk bottle and then rummaged in the cupboard for a few biscuits. He plonked himself down next to Olivia, who gave the contents of the pot a stir and poured out the tea.

Queenie lapped up the remains of her tea as she listened carefully to what Olivia had to say. Her eyes grew wide as Olivia explained about all the research she'd done and how the document would be very unlikely to stand up in court because of the way matters had been conducted. When she came to the part where she said that the bad men could even be made to pay Archie some money, that their wicked scheme could backfire on them completely, Queenie added her support with loud barks. Duke and Kat joined in, Valentino and Queenie Two emerged from the front room and did their bit and even Old Soldier put in an appearance from behind the cooker, adding his contribution to the racket.

'We could threaten them with the police unless they pay up,' said Olivia, clapping her hands.

'Isn't that blackmail?' said Archie, doubtfully.

'Probably,' said Olivia. 'But, so what? They deserve it.'

Queenie upped her barking to show her approval of the plan. The others followed suit.

'All right, all right,' said Archie, covering his ears. 'I'll think about it. Anything to make these dogs shut their traps.'

As if by magic, the dogs all stopped their barking.

'Well, that settles it, I suppose,' said Archie. 'I'll get Nick down here and tell him.'

51. Kat Helps the Plan Along

KAT

I paw at Olivia's feet and she picks me up and tickles my head. 'Go on, Granddad. Phone Uncle Nick now.'

Archie picks up the phone and dials a number. He doesn't sound at all friendly. 'Get yourself down here now, lad,' he says. 'No, I don't mean in an hour. I mean now. No arguments.' He puts the phone down.

'Well done, Granddad,' says Olivia. 'Now you need to stick to the script. You need to say that you've consulted a solicitor and that what he and those men did was illegal and that you want compensation. We'll put it like that. If he quibbles, then you say something like you wouldn't like to have to involve the police, that they all risk a spell in prison if you report them. You have to be strict, Granddad. Understood?'

I feel very proud of Olivia and give her face a lick, but she's looking anxiously at Archie and barely notices. Archie seems worried. 'I'm not sure I can do it, Olivia,' he says.

'You can, Granddad,' says Olivia. 'We're all behind you, aren't we, dogs?' She looks round at Queenie, Duke, Queenie Two and Valentino and they all bark. I join in too, but I still sound a little squeaky, with my being only a youngster. Olivia smiles down at me. 'I'm sure you're going to be a lot of help, Kat,' she says. 'You tell that nasty Old Nick when he comes that we're not standing for any nonsense.'

Archie laughs and goes and pours himself a whisky and lemonade. 'Dutch courage,' he says to Olivia as he lifts his glass and gulps it down.

***

'Be on your guard, Kat,' says Queenie. 'Nick is bound to try and wriggle out of things. We may need to intervene.'

'How do you mean, Queenie?'

'She means you may need to perform a little spell,' says Duke. 'Discreetly, of course,' he adds, glancing at Queenie. 'You two are the only ones that can change the outcome if things start to go badly.'

'Hark at Mr Serious here,' says Queenie, 'finally realizing that this is no joking matter.'

'I don't know about that, Queen,' says Duke, looking uncomfortable. 'You gotta laugh in life even when there doesn't seem much to laugh about.'

'We'll have to change your name to Duke the Philosopher instead of Duke the Dog Guardian,' says Queenie.

'Just stick with Duke,' he growls. 'Now who's not taking things seriously?'

'Keep the noise down, will you?' yells Archie from the bedroom, where he's gone to practise his speech. 'I can't hear myself think.'

Olivia and I are at the bedroom door, watching him. He looks funny, looking at himself sternly in the mirror and muttering.

'You'll be fine, Granddad,' says Olivia. 'Just be yourself.'

***

There's a knock at the kitchen door and Old Nick pokes his head round. 'You there, Dad?' he says.

'I'm here, lad,' says Archie, coming out of the bedroom. 'Now, you listen here. This sale isn't happening. Got it? It's illegal and we want compensation. So you can tell those lackeys of yours that they'd better pay up, or else.'

Olivia's nodding behind him.

'What?' says Old Nick. 'Don't be daft, Dad. They've got copies of those papers. It's all above board.'

'Oh no it isn't,' says Archie. 'We've spoken to a solicitor and it's entrapment, that's what it is.'

Olivia's eyebrows go up. *Entrapment*? she mouths at him. He looks away.

'But…' splutters Old Nick.

'But nothing,' says Archie. 'You're a disgrace to the name Truelove and, if you don't want to go to prison, you'd best make sure those villains cough up. You tricked me.'

'I know you didn't want to sell, Dad, but it'll be better in the long run for you and Olivia. You'll see. I didn't want to sell either, but what with debts and…'

I feel Olivia going stiff. She's going to get all upset again. I know it. I shut my eyes hard and a little ditty comes into my head:

'*Where there is doubt,*
'*The truth will out.*
'*Tell one more lie,*
'*And you may die.*'

I open my eyes and stare at Nick. He stops mid-sentence.

'Debt? What debt?' says Archie. 'I've never owed anybody any money in my life. Look at me when I'm talking to you.'

I'm staring straight into Nick's eyes. He can't look away.

'No, you're right, Dad, there is no debt,' he stutters. 'I…I…'

'You what…? Spit it out, lad. You what…?'

'It was all Ma's idea. I wanted to help Felix.'

'Felix? What are you talking about, lad? What's Felix got to do with it?

'Look at me, boy,' says Archie, giving him a shove. 'How's your mother involved in all this… this chicanery?'

My power over Nick is broken as he steps back and looks at Archie.

'No, nothing. It's got nothing to do with Felix. Nor Ma. It's…'

I give a warning bark and Nick glances my way. I lock eyes with him and repeat my little ditty in my head. He goes pale. 'I can get compensation for you, Dad. How much d'you want?'

Archie glances at Olivia. She mouths something. 'A thousand pounds,' he says. Nick nods and Olivia pokes Archie in the back. 'I mean five thousand,' he says. 'I want at least five thousand pounds.'

'I'll get it for you, Dad.'

I almost feel sorry for Nick. He looks like he might cry. He turns tail and heads for the door.

'I want it by tonight,' yells Archie.

Nick pauses, turns and points at me. 'That dog's contaminated,' he says as he stumbles out of the door, 'contaminated.'

52. A Happy Ending

Kat

So, you see, I really am a magic dog.

That same night, Old Nick comes back and shoves a lot of bits of paper at Archie, mumbling that he's sorry and that he didn't mean any harm. Archie tells him he isn't forgiven yet – I should think not! - but shakes his hand anyway. He tells him that he's never to try anything like that again and to keep Pookah away from the place, that she's not to come down here again. Queenie, Duke and the others all cheer. I keep a close eye on Nasty Nick, but he keeps his eyes off me and soon leaves, looking miserable. But that's how he always looks anyway.

Archie and Olivia dance around the kitchen, throwing the bits of paper into the air and shouting *Five thousand pounds!*, and then laugh and hug each other. All the dogs join in with barking, but not dancing, as they're probably still a bit sore. Olivia holds me up in the air and moves me around in time to the music, which is coming from her phone.

It feels a happy time.

Queenie was very pleased with me when I told her about my little ditties. Even Duke was nice to me. You're a star, Kat Rat, he says. When I fluff out my coat and say that I feel I can do anything, Queenie tells me not to get cocky, that I still have a lot to learn. Malina's still out there, she says, so we can't let our guard down. She's wagging her tail though, so I think she's really happy with the way things have turned out. Duke raises his eyebrows.

Olivia says they must use the money to 'spruce the place up'. I imagine that probably means painting and mending things to make everywhere look nice. I don't know why. I like it the way it is. Archie nods and tells her she's a grand lass, none better. I nod, because she's my best friend and we're always going to be together and do lots of good things, like Aurora said.

Do you feel guilty at all, Granddad? Olivia asks Archie. Archie thinks for a moment and then says, Not in the slightest. You? Not in the slightest, she replies, and they both burst out laughing and hug each other again.

We all go to bed early, after all the bits of paper have been gathered up, and Archie doesn't say anything about me sleeping with Olivia. Duke and Valentino make themselves comfortable on the floor of her bedroom.

Before Queenie goes in with Archie, she turns to look at us all and nods. You've done well today, she says. Tomorrow's another day. Let's see what that brings.

I think Queenie's very wise and I hope, one day, I'll be as wise as her.

In the meantime, See you soon, everybody.

Author Note
About Jo

Jo is the author of *Kat the Dog*, the first in the *Kat the Dog* series.

She has been writing for the last twenty years. This is her first published novel.

A graduate in modern languages from Leeds University, Jo has translated a number of books from French and Italian, including: *Dogs of the World; The Book of Practical Astrology; UFO, The Bermuda Triangle, Atlantis; Cartomancy.*

Jo has spent practically her whole life around animals and often used to walk up to twenty rescue dogs at a time, sometimes with a goat in tow. She wasn't terribly popular with other dogwalkers in the area, but that's not something that keeps her awake at night.

Having lived and worked abroad and in London for a number of years, she is now firmly settled back in the North of England with her two Jack Russells, who give her a dog's life. She loves purple, is a fan of all things magical and would like to be able to fly.

To find out more about Kat the Dog, visit www.katthedog.co.uk

If you would like to know when the next book in the series is coming out, please sign up to Kat Klub on the website for the occasional newsletter and a free copy of the short story *Archie's First Dog*.

Acknowledgements

Thank you to Doug for editing my initial drafts of *Kat the Dog* and *Kat and the Killer Dog* and for his patience and ideas.

Thank you to the Writers Advice Centre for their appraisal and useful advice.

Thank you to Eleanor at Jericho Writers for her insightful report and suggestions.

Many thanks to Sarah for being prepared to read through the manuscript more than once and recommending a substantial change of direction for Book One.

Thanks to Paul for his (reluctant) editing. But then he's not a huge fan of dogs and most definitely not magic, so it was probably quite a chore.

Thanks to Jericho Writers for their helpful videos on all aspects of writing and publishing.

Many thanks to Ken of Creative Covers for his beautiful book cover and illustrations, his dedication and helpful suggestions.

A big shout out to Eevi Jones for generously sharing her extremely helpful videos on writing and publishing Children's books.

Thank you to Wendy and Olivia for their continued support and encouragement.

And finally, my biggest thank you goes to all the dogs, who've been, and continue to be, in my life, for their loyal friendship and companionship over many years. They are my inspiration.

Glossary

A

Ain't: the verb 'to be' in all its forms, e.g. 'I ain't' = 'I'm not'; You ain't' = 'you're not'.
Best to stick with the normal forms of the verb 'to be' if you don't want people to give you funny looks (no offence to Queenie and Duke)

Amulet: a charm against evil, e.g. a necklace

Approaching one's Prime: getting to the best and most productive time of one's life, perhaps not strictly true in Archie's case

Artlessly: usually innocently, but in Katja's case, there may be a little manipulation

B

Baggin time: a short period devoted to tea (and occasionally coffee) and possibly a cheese and jam sandwich

Banter (n.): exchange of insults, in the nicest possible way

Barrage Balloon: a large balloon fixed to the ground, which, in the context of a person or dog, implies they are a little plump

Belt up: a not-so-polite form of 'please be quiet'

Bird-brained: daft

Blarting duffer: a person or dog who talks a lot and loudly about things they don't know much about

Bloomin(g): a word used to express annoyance

A **Bob**: a shilling, the equivalent of 5p in today's money

Brindle: tawny colour with streaks

Butty: sandwich (usually made with jam and cheese, especially if you're Archie)

C

Caboodle: a large collection of things or people. Sometimes called 'Kit and Caboodle'

In **Cahoots** with: conspiring with somebody to be up to no good

Calibre: the (high) quality of a person/dog

Camouflage (v.): conceal, hide

Casing the joint: checking out a place, usually with a plan to commit a crime like theft

Channel (v.): allow a spirit or entity to speak through you

Like **Cheese at Fourpence**: hanging around, wasting time

Chicanery: deception; skullduggery (good word!)

Chunter: mutter

Clink (n.): slang for prison

Codger: an old man (an affectionate term if said by Queenie about Archie)

Codswallop: nonsense, rather like 'poppycock'

Contaminated: polluted, corrupt

Old Coot: old man, who may or may not be daft. A bit of an insult (unless said by Queenie about Archie)

D

Decorum: proper and polite behaviour

Decrepit: weakened by old age, feeble

Discombobulated: baffled (permanent state of dim dogs), puzzled

A **Doddle**: something that is very easy to do

Doglore: a set of rules governing the standards and behaviour of dogs

The Dog's Boll…: short for a rude word, so best forget about that one

Dogwalla: person who likes dogs (in Archiespeak)

Dollop: chunk or blob

E

Enlightened: somebody who's 'seen the light', a bit of a clever clogs.

F

To send somebody off with a **Flea in their Ear**: angrily tell somebody to go away

Feign: pretend

Fob off: tell somebody something to stop them asking questions

A **Footling Dandy**: a boy/man, who prats around the place, thinking he's important when he isn't, often dressed in fancy clothes

Fracking: a method of obtaining gas and oil from rocks (very much disapproved of by the inhabitants of Kymera, particularly Archie, because the dogs don't really understand it)

Fray: battle

Fripperies: unimportant trivial things

Frisson: shiver, shudder, tingle

Fuddy-duddy: old-fashioned fussy person/dog

Not to be the **Full Ticket**: not quite with it; could be used about the dim dogs

G

Gallivanting: going around and about having a good time

Gargoyle: grotesque, ugly creature

Gawping: staring

Gawky: awkward, clumsy

Gormless gobbin: a stupid-looking person/dog

Gotta: got to (lazy form)

Gnashers: teeth

Grand: a word Archie often uses to mean 'great/super'

Green-eyed monster: jealousy

H

Hackles: hairs sticking up on the back of a dog

Harrumph (v.): noisily clear throat

Henchbitch: follower/helper (not in a good way)

Hoo-ha: fuss

I

Ignoramus: an ignorant person or dog

Inkling: a suspicion or idea

'**In season**': the time when a girl dog is able to have babies

J

A **Jimmy riddle**: a wee, a term used by people like Archie, as in 'I'm going for a Jimmy Riddle', rhyming slang for 'piddle'

L

La Lupina: the most important dog in the entire universe

'**Let's be having you**': 'Come on, hurry up'

Loll around: lie about looking lazy, possibly with your tongue hanging out (mainly if you're a dog)

Lovesick parrot: a parrot in love

Luminosity: brightness; glow

Lummox: an affectionate insult (when used by Queenie)

M

Makeshift: temporary

La Malina: the worst, horriblest dog in the entire universe

Manky: dirty, scruffy

Maudlin: soppy and sentimental

Meticulous: showing close attention to detail

Minions: groupies; inferior beings or dogs or fairies

Mollified: placated, calmed, soothed

Mutt: a dog of mixed breed (insult)

N

Nab (v.): catch

Nag: old, feeble horse (not of course true in Oberon's case)

Nincompoop: a silly person or dog

A **No-Brainer**: something that's obvious, like 'everybody loves cheese' (well I know I do)

Not a Dicky Bird: nothing (old-fashioned)

Nowt: nothing

Nowty: bad-tempered

Numbskull: a stupid person/dog, a bit like the dim dogs

O

Owt: anything

P

Parasite: a person or dog who lives off other people

Parched: very thirsty

'**Penny for them**': asking what somebody is thinking (but not wanting to pay very much to know)

Phwoar: a strong expression of (in this case) distaste

Piffle: nonsense

Polite Conversation: socially correct, stilted, shallow, not very interesting talking

Pooh Pooh (v.): dismiss something as silly

Poppycock: nonsense, rather like 'codswallop'

Preen: admire oneself

Pride and Prejudice: a romantic novel/film, very popular with Olivia and Queenie

Puny: small and weak

Q

Quibble: complain, argue

R

Reet: right, proper

Riled up: cross, annoyed

Rite of passage: a major event in a person or dog's life

Rollicking: a severe telling-off

Rue: regret

Rummage (v.): poke about; root around

Runt: the weakest of the litter, not really a compliment, or at least Kat doesn't think so

S

To be a '**Sandwich short of a picnic**': to be a bit stupid, like the dim dogs

Scurry: move quickly with short, quick steps

Shifty: false and untrustworthy

Shyster: an unscrupulous person

Skedaddle: depart quickly

Slimeball: an unpleasant, insincere person

Slope (v.): move aimlessly/lazily, usually followed by 'off'

Socialized: made to fit in with polite society

Spark out: unconscious

Spring chicken: a young person (or dog in this case)

Spruce up: smarten

Staffie: Staffordshire bull terrier

Stupiditis: a state of being very stupid

Swilling your face off: having a wash, usually Archie when he's cooling down

T

Take a shine to someone/something: like a person/dog immediately

Tedious: boring, dull

Toe the line: obey the rules

Togs: clothes

Turn a blind eye: pretend not to notice

Turntable: a rotating object for playing old records on

Twaddle: nonsense

U

Under the Influence: suffering from the effects of alcohol, probably whisky

W

Wheedle: talk to someone in a silly, whiny voice

Willy-nilly: in a disorganised way

Wuthering Heights: romantic book/film about doomed love (firm favourite with Olivia and the dogs)

Printed in Dunstable, United Kingdom

82595306R00211